WOO-WOO

TRUE STORIES OF MAGIC, MIRACLES & INFINITE POSSIBILITIES

MELISSA MCCANN-TILTON   JO ALBERTSON

CHRISTY JAYNES   MICHELLE SAVAGE   DEANNA COX

MICHELLE KRISS   SHAY MICHELLE DRAPEAU

CARRIE QUINTANILLA   NATASHA CAMPISI

SULIT
PRESS

Paperback: 9798993092904

Ebook: 9798990575394

Edited by Avery Toomes and Michelle Savage

Cover art by Ian Koviak

Sulit Press

www.suitpress.com

CONTENTS

ABOUT SULIT PRESS

Sulit Press is a boutique publishing house that provides high-touch support to thought leaders, industry shakers, and changemakers writing impactful nonfiction. Whether you're publishing a personal memoir, an industry-specific solo book, or contributing to a collaborative multi-author book, we help you go from aspiring author to published author—with clarity, confidence, and community.

Founder and CEO Michelle Savage is an international best-selling author, speaker, and mentor who helps high-vibe, heart-centered women share and amplify their stories. With a background in publishing, coaching, and storytelling, Michelle is passionate about helping women turn their lived experience into professional assets—whether that means a book, a brand, or a bigger platform.

She's led women through their first published pieces, hosted sold-out retreats, and built a thriving community of bold, generous authors who are ready to be seen.

Want to learn more? Visit www.sulitpress.com

INTRODUCTION

Only two things divide a skeptic from a mystic: the first is the need for proof, and the second is direct experience.

For many of us, whether we've stopped demanding proof or witnessed the strange and the wondrous firsthand, reality isn't fixed at all, but a layered, shifting landscape.

Often the term *woo-woo* is used as a kind of disclaimer, a warning before we share something others might judge us for. After all, we are serious people. We have jobs, families, responsibilities. We've seen the eye rolls when the conversation turns mystical, and we've also seen the over-the-top stereotypes of those who proudly claim the title as if it were their whole personality. No shade on them—do your thing and whatnot.

For some of us, mystical moments appear in our lives whether we seek them out or not, leaving us open to a reality that is stranger, more layered, and often more beautiful than we were taught to expect.

The women in this book know that territory well. Their stories cannot be measured or tested, but they are true accounts of what they lived. You will read about an unexpected brush with the astral plane, a near-death experience, visitations from loved ones who have passed, manifestations that defy explanation, and guidance that led one author back to God.

From ghost stories to divine guidance, leaning into the "woo" is no longer an apology; it's a reclamation.

We hope this book serves as a dazzling reminder that magic and mystery are always present when we choose to look.

1

WOO-SHIT

BY MELISSA MCCANN-TILTON

W hen I walked into the room, her tits were out.

She was propped up in an adjustable bed, sheets wrapped loosely around her waist, a diaper hidden beneath them. *Hide the diaper, show the tits.* She looked like a great yogi in a loincloth. Her hair was piled into a messy bun on top of her head. She'd drawn on eyebrows and eyelashes with a ballpoint pen—but not where you'd expect. They circled her areolas like little acts of defiance or final expressions of freedom. We were so buttoned up. Now we were letting it all spill out, beautiful and horrifying.

Her breasts were perfect. Round. Full. Alive. Even as the rest of her body disappeared. Later, I found out they were fake. She was 49 years old, 5'8", and weighed 86 pounds. She was evaporating.

When her husband called, I couldn't comprehend it. Just a few weeks earlier, we were planning a concert. She had just come back from vacation in Hawaii. She looked small to me—but I was with her so often, I adjusted my perception. I made it positive.

We didn't talk about her cancer. I hoped it was getting better. I was too afraid to ask. We were swimming in it, saying nothing. Like treading water in a vast pool of poison—just avert your eyes. Don't notice anything is changing. Speaking it into the universe would make it too real.

So we stayed silent. Don't name it. Don't feed it. Don't give it light. Maybe then it won't grow.

He said to come tomorrow. She's being transferred to hospice. We're down to days. Are we still not talking about it? I guess we're talking about it now. It's become undeniable. In all our ignore-ance—our practiced silence—it grew massive. Too big to comprehend. It was consuming all of us. I woke up in a daze.

I have to go see my friend today.

I have to.

I get to.

I want to.

I don't want to.

Jesus, this is heavy.

How do you look someone in the eyes and wonder: *Is this the last time I'll ever see you alive?*

Maybe not. But maybe.

She has something she needs to tell me. My mind spiraled into self-mythology: *She needs me to do something.* (I love to do things. Do, do, do, do, do.)

She's going to give me something. A purpose. A message.

So fucking selfish.

She's going to tell me there's something wrong with me.

That she's seen it—some illness in my body, some fracture in my psyche. That she knows something I don't.

Death doesn't just confront the dying. It confronts the mirrors around them. We're all sitting here before this great death, seeing what we see through our own small, terrified windows. They say there's a gift in death. Lessons we should be grateful for.

Bullshit. This sucks. And it's heavy.

It's bigger than anything I've ever had to lift—and that's saying something.

I better go get ready.

No mascara.

What the hell makes a good *death visit outfit?*

My god.

It's a nice facility.

I suppose there are all flavors of hospice—ranging from bleak holding chambers for families who can't afford proper care or can't bear to do it themselves... to places like this. *Nice facilities.* The kind with manicured lawns and union landscaping crews. From the outside, it looks like a retirement center—harmless, pleasant, forgettable.

The entrance reminds me of a church lobby. An elderly woman mans the guest sign-in desk like a solemn usher. For a moment, I feel like I should offer something—a prayer, a tithe. A piece of myself.

Her husband came to get us. Guided us through hallways that revealed hospital rooms, beeping, groaning. Then there's a playground. Right in the middle of all this is a lovely garden with rhododendrons in full bloom, a little waterfall, butterflies flitting around, and a playground right in the center. That's depressing. In past scenarios, I would have thought how nice for the grandkids, but this is the KIDS. I want to burst into tears before I even reach her room. But then I look at her husband. He looks exhausted—haunted. Like a zombie going through motions, following protocol, curating her experience one quiet instruction at a time.

We get to room 15, and I just walk in. No waiting, why bother, here we go. There she is—with her tits. My husband trails behind me. She looks up to reveal lips full of red lipstick and a look that says, I did this for you bitch. And she did. She required her husband to go to the store before our arrival and find the reddest lipstick he could. Her painting was so juxtaposed, so bizarre when compared with her skeletal frame and compromised position. It was so polished. After a moment, we just started to laugh. It's ridiculousness, indeed, the ridiculousness of this entire thing was comical. Sad, yes, but also just *what-the-fuck?*

It's her death, not mine.

But it is mine.

It's all of ours.

The red lipstick? It was mine—for a moment. Then it wasn't. Later, she told someone else a story about the red lipstick. And just like that, it became theirs.

She was finally getting proper medical care. The proper notion is part of the grander debate here, but I was finally comfortable that a fair amount of Western medicine had been added to the miracle regimen. Admittedly, far too late to have any impact on her living.

Dilaudid was onboard, making her loopy. Her dose had worn off while she slept, so we were playing a little catch-up. I could tell she was hurting, but not nearly as much as the last time we were together in her living room. She could hardly function then.

Her mouth was dry, and she wanted hard candy. I held her after we stopped laughing about her lipstick. She was warm, too warm. She told me to get my emotions out, so we went from laughing to crying. I sat next to her hospital bed in a little fold-out metal chair with my hand on her arm. She told me the things she needed me to hear.

Our husband's left to pick up take-out. We spent a good deal of time considering our nourishment. Food was off the table until now. She literally couldn't eat. With the Dilaudid she's feeling good enough to taste. We considered the options and settled on my favorite food: nachos. I recognized that she was planning her final suppers around *our* favorite foods.

When the husbands left, she spoke again—more urgently now, more freely. About what I was meant to do next.

Help women, she said.

She wants me to help women. It was like a cry for help she hadn't known how to articulate in life. A final offering of what she hadn't said before. Some expression of her own unmet needs, passed to me in the form of a mission.

She seemed disappointed. Exhausted. There was a depth of resentment in her voice when she spoke of Joel, her husband. She never mentioned it before—not once. I think she knew if she had, I would've judged her. I would've seen it as selfish. This man was turning himself inside out for you!

So she swallowed it.

She shoved it deep down—into her bowels, maybe.

Why couldn't she just say: *This is what I need?*

I cry and tell her how I feel.

She's talking nonsense now. It's the drugs, of course—but maybe not entirely. Maybe these fragments are coming from somewhere deep inside her. She says she wants a warehouse.

In one room, women can smash things.

In another, they fix things.

And in the final room, I talk to them.

She's in a loop, falling in and out of sleep, spilling out her inner thoughts in fragments that sometimes make sense and sometimes don't. Nothing has changed.

Just two weeks ago, I walked into her bedroom at home one last time. I had no idea it would be the last time I walked into that room with her alive.

She was curled on her side—the only position she could manage. Her hair was piled atop her head, regal and undone. She looked impossibly small. It was a picture of what was coming. She was in a great deal of pain. She patted the space beside her. An invitation.

I laid down on the bed beside her. She had been having visions. The veil was thin. She told me about these containers, jars. She told me they held these pieces of her life. I didn't understand. I thought it was the pain. She started talking about helping women then. The loop had begun weeks earlier. She was gathering information, preparing for her journey, I just didn't get it yet. She told me she saw us at some conference. She was on stage, speaking. "It doesn't have to be this way. Life can be full of love. Of growth. Of magic."

Joel and Chuck roll in with a great aluminum boat of nachos.

She lies on her stomach, propped on this pillow under her breasts. I lay the food out in front of her on the bed with a towel beneath, and we dive in. It's like the final supper. Cheese-drenched, soggy chips, humid from the foil box. It's not gourmet. It's sloppy. It's not bad, but it's certainly not good. I don't really feel like eating it, but I eat it. She's diving in, scooping sour cream and salsa, dripping on the bed.

It's sloppy. It's ridiculous. It's holy.

Now she's more alert now from the food, and Chuck, my husband, starts teasing her about the lawn people. There are about 15 lawn service men wandering around the courtyard, trimming and blowing things. They're deeply diligent. Chuck speculates that the diligence is related to her tasteful side boob. I mean, you must not get much hot chick boob action in the courtyard of the hospice center.

This was... different. Out of place. *Tragically hot.*

She finds this funny on the meds and goes for it. She's flirting with the lawn crew. Raising up enough to be provocative or at least enough to make us laugh. She really is so funny. Basic funny. *Raunchy*. I'll miss that. We make fun of the guy blowing leaves outside her window.

"I thought he just blew those leaves the other direction." Chuck says, "He needed a better angle."

Then we sit quietly. The laughter fades. The loop begins again. We get bored, uncomfortable. I start studying the furniture—hunter green with tiny flowers, straight out of a 1980s Holiday Inn. The nightstands are beat to hell from weary wives and husbands sitting with the dying. The art looks like it came from a Home Goods fire sale. There are lights from the bed on the floor, indicators. Surprisingly, there are very few machines, not many beeps. I guess you don't need to heavily monitor imminent death.

She had cancer for a year before she told me. An entire year.

I would've called her first. She would've been my first call. But she kept it from me. She wasn't getting standard Western treatment. The chemo, the radiation weren't for her. She must have known I wouldn't approve.

Instead, she was doing "Woo-Shit." She didn't call it that. She started talking about Woo before I knew she had cancer. She began telling me fantastical stories of radical healing, superhuman powers, chi, life-force, kundalini. We had eye-rolling arguments about it. Her saying I could reverse my Hashimoto's disease and cure my anxiety with this woo.

Come on. She'd lost it.

What I didn't know was that she was doing Woo-Shit to cure the cancer. But mostly, I didn't know she had the cancer, just that my friend was acting strangely. All this woo...just showed

8

up, like an uninvited guest replacing me. I'd seen the Woo-World before—but only from a distance. I judged it. A mess of meandering, patchouli-wearing hippies clinging to fantasies. It was fantastical. It was illogical.

This woo felt like a betrayal. We were both atheists. We believed in science. As a child, I had been beaten in the name of god routinely, like it was cleaning up the dinner dishes. Religion was filthy to me. No god was coming to help.

My childhood trauma had left me with a heavy dose of panic attacks. I popped Xanax and Zofran just to function. And I did —function. I kept going. I was high-performing. No one knew. One of the deepest connections Kris and I shared was our childhood trauma. We had both made it "out." We had both been abused. It was a quiet, knowing bond between us.

But my particular kind of abuse further cemented my bias against God.

I grew up as transient as those woo-shit hippies I mocked— bouncing from town to town in an olive-green Pinto, often sleeping in the hatchback. My father was brilliant, charismatic. Both of my parents were highly educated. Masters, PhD...in theology. Religion was their medium of influence. I watched him overtake a congregation, a commune, gather his sheep and take what he desired. I saw firsthand the seductive power of religion. Its manipulation. Its darkness.

I saw the helplessness of these lambs as they longed for meaning, for guidance. I saw the same behavior pattern in business as my career grew. It wasn't so different from this religious conquest. Entering with pretty words, accomplishments, credibility, then taking what I desired for my own survival, my own power. This dance with the lambs that they seem unaware of, lost to. It struck me how conscious I was of this power and how unconscious the lambs were of the taking of it. The perversion of such an innocent hope. I watched how my father enjoyed it, the ravaging.

So when Kris turned to the woo—when she placed her hope in unseen forces and healing frequencies and divine energy—I didn't just roll my eyes.

I flinched.

Because to me, that wasn't light. That wasn't liberation or faith or love.

It was the same trap.

The same illusion.

Just dressed in crystals instead of crosses.

So yes—we were abused. We were disconnected from God. But we weren't unique.

So many women experience this damage as children, as adults. We were only unique in our circles. You simply didn't talk about this kind of thing in the worlds we lived in, and it connected us. We were successful, beautiful, *totally normal*. We were both at the top of multi-million-dollar businesses. We were problem solvers, keeper goers, doers.

We survived through carefully constructed compartmentalization, dissociation, disconnection. We performed, and we recognized the performance in each other. It wasn't exactly a kinship, more of an exposure.

Oh god, you actually see me.

We had both carefully constructed images. I remember her describing her cancer diagnosis at age forty-seven. She said, "No one would have ever guessed." She was so healthy looking. There was so much venere, a parade of carefully constructed outfits, orders, and interactions. No one would have ever guessed about any of it. We were both women who deeply understood defilement and somehow used it in our favor. We understood the dance and were comfortable with its dirtiness. We knew no other way.

Women like us weren't supposed to be in the same room together.

I met her at work. We were both beautiful and young, ambitious and aggressive. We were both too big in our own ways. It's difficult for two big, ambitious, beautiful women to share space. Our world has taught us there's only room for one, so we try to kill each other. It's some subconscious rule, instinctual, survival. And completely false and unnecessary.

My husband was the one who pushed the friendship. He saw something in both of us—something connected. He saw past our learned need to consume each other for our personal power. He sensed the shared history before we could name it: something hard, something dirty, something we had both survived.

Had we actually made it out?

By society's standards, we were blazing success stories. Neither of us talked about how we got there. And when we did, people retreated. Our truth made us even more terrifying.

We became distantly intrigued by each other. Then my husband did it—he invited them on vacation with us. I hadn't even had dinner out with this couple before. They had never been to my house, and I hadn't been to theirs. Our first get-to-know-you would be full frontal. No toe-dipping, no polite sniffing around. We were diving in.

Honestly, it's bizarre to think about it now. I can't remember a single meaningful social interaction with them before that trip. Just one thing: after my son was born, she sent him a tiny tracksuit—delivered through my husband. I remember feeling suspicious.

Why would this woman be nice to me?

But that wasn't about her. I was suspicious of *anyone* who was nice to me. If you were kind, you wanted something. But she didn't seem to need anything from me. Which made the gesture even more suspicious.

We had a shared workspace. Maybe that was enough to justify the leap. People at work reacted to us with the same mix of awe and discomfort—just from different angles. I was louder, more overtly dominant. She was quieter, more precise. She didn't speak often, but when she did, people listened. She was aloof. I was a bulldozer.

Both of us were unreachable in our own ways—closed off, defenses sky-high, masked in superiority and bound by pain we hadn't named. We were hard as rocks.

Men responded with some blend of desire and fear. Women were just mean behind our backs and sometimes directly to our faces.

She was distant. I was a bully. And we both buried ourselves in work to avoid facing ourselves.

So there we were—on our annual beach vacation. This time, it was Mexico. Palomas in hand, kids running barefoot through the sand. She had two boys. I had three, plus a baby girl. We'd come for two weeks—my idea. I'd pushed for a longer break post-COVID, a chance to reconnect. But something was different. She felt distant. Withheld. And I was about to find out why.

"I've been diagnosed with cancer," she said. "The kids don't know."

What?

I cried. I hugged her—but not really. It was our usual kind of hug: quick, upper-shoulders only, then a push away. Disconnected. Guarded. There was love behind it, but not in it.

"Jesus, Kris. I'm so sorry."

I couldn't ask any more questions. I was afraid to know the answers. It was so fast—like she'd told me she broke a fingernail. I was reeling, but immediately trying to pull it together. We had to get back up to the house. We'd been gone too long. There were things to do. We were keeper-goers.

We walked back to the house like nothing had happened. I held this information for the entire vacation. I didn't want to wreck my husband. I couldn't drop it on my kids; her own kids didn't even know. I didn't want to acknowledge it to her husband. He would have just fallen apart. So I compartmentalized, and she compartmentalized. It was so natural, effortless.

The information boiled inside me as we went about our leisure. We swam and dined. We rode waves and played with unaware children. It felt surreal—going through the motions of a beach vacation while carrying the weight of her secret.

Before I fully grasped the *woo-shit* she was chasing, it began revealing itself—not as a concept, but as a force. A rupture.

Something that spilled from the spirit realm into the physical world, whether I wanted it to or not.

It was June, on the west coast of Mexico. A tiny town north of Zihuatanejo—you know, the beach from *The Shawshank Redemption*. That iconic scene. Ultimate freedom.

We rode bikes to the restaurant, bikes in Mexican disrepair, wobbly and janky but still moving forward. Like us. We sat in heavy wooden chairs, ordered slow-coming food, the way it always is there. She wasn't drinking—couldn't. Instead, she ordered a giant coconut. The waiter hacked the top off, stuck in a straw. She sipped it like communion.

The weather was listening to my internal chaos. A Mexican grandma was conjuring spirits on the beach. What was she doing? She stood in the sand near the ocean and waved her arms wildly, chanting loudly. Kris was mesmerized. I was unnerved.

And then—everything flipped. Literally.

The heavy wooden chairs started toppling. Food flew off tables. A hurricane was hovering just offshore—not directly striking, but close enough to knock us sideways. It was absurd, cinematic. The husbands sent us to the bikes—they'd handle the food. Because of course they would. Because nothing was happening, right?

Let's just finish dinner.

We ran to the damaged bikes and hopped on. They worked well enough. The rain was a deluge. The storm was a deluge, shopkeepers scrambling to shutter their storefronts. We were going faster than I was comfortable with. Transformers burst above our heads, sparks flying, the sky splitting open. The world was exploding. It was pouring out of me. And for whatever reason, it was *hilarious*.

I rode behind her, and there she was—one hand on the handlebars, the other gripping her sacred fucking coconut.

It was *insane*. It made no sense.

We're trying to make it back to our vacation house and save this coconut. We're not giving it up. I'm squealing and laughing and trying to stay afloat. She keeps looking back to take care of *me*. "Keep laughing! As long as I can hear your laugh, I know you're alive," she grinned and yelled over her shoulder. The paradox seemed to miss its target. We all arrived...alive for now, drenched. I've never been more wet in my life. I could have sat in the center of the ocean and been drier. We sat with towels, eating out of styrofoam containers while the pool overflowed. The hurricane hadn't just come from the sky. It had come from *within*. It was coming out whether we allowed it or not.

We returned from the hurricane, and down the rabbit hole we went. I was a reluctant convert. Fighting all the way. Clinging to my compartmentalization. I had certainly done yoga and meditation before, but this was different. I was furious, and then I furiously participated. What else was I supposed to do?

The fantastical thinking was abundant. Stories of miraculous recoveries. Modern-day manifesting. My father used to call this *the gospel of prosperity*—a perversion of faith that twisted suffering into a transaction. It was manipulation dressed as hope. It felt intentionally disrespectful. Desperate.

We started going to meditation retreats—weeklong intensives where we logged fifty hours of stillness like some kind of spiritual marathon. At times, it felt eerily familiar—like the cultish environment of my childhood. People were eager, desperate, waving their mystical résumés around like business cards.

"I'm clairvoyant. I'm clairaudient. I can read minds." (*Aren't those the same thing?*)

This world felt strange, bizarre...and familiar. I felt like a jerk for judging her, and I also felt desperate. I just wanted to be near her, even if I thought it was crazy making. I tried to stay grounded in science. That was my anchor. I knew the studies. The breathwork. The neural regulation. I could explain meditation in peer-reviewed language. I had *no* intention of becoming spiritual.

It seemed...ridiculous.

Weak-minded.

But then—shit started happening.

It was one of the first meditations, thousands of us in a massive hall, thick with divine feminine desperation—I dropped in. I followed the script—breath, silence, awareness. And suddenly— I could feel every heart in the room. Not metaphorically. *Physically.*

It was overwhelming. Terrifying.

I needed to believe it was bullshit. Woo-shit. I needed to believe I was falling for some elaborate groupthink manipulation.

But I wasn't so sure.

Kris, by now, was fully immersed. She found her people—soft, glowing women who said yes, who mirrored her light, who worshipped her radiance. People who made her feel good. Safe. Untouchable.

I wasn't that kind of friend. I asked questions. I raised eyebrows. I wasn't open—not really. I needed space. Eighteen inches to ten feet. I didn't like being touched. I would recoil without thinking. It was an embedded response—trauma wired into muscle memory. My boundaries weren't just emotional; they were anatomical. Still, I resented the pulling away. I knew I made it hard to stay close. But I didn't want to be left behind.

So we did this dance.

I'd inch into the woo—just close enough to feel the resistance rise in me, the cynicism, the shame of my own disbelief. I'd roll my eyes. I'd dig in my heels. And then—just when I was ready to write it all off—something would happen. A flicker. A crack in the armor. A moment of undeniable presence. Something that felt like magic.

Not hers. Not mine.

Ours.

And then, one night, she invited me into something deeper.

A home gathering. Some kind of meditation. Crystal bowls? Drums? She never gave me much detail—just enough to get me to show up. That was her way. Let the mystery pull me forward. I didn't care what it was. I would do anything to be near her while she was dying. So I agreed.

As the evening approached, my resistance became overwhelming. "I'm not going to go." My husband encouraged me. "You won't look back on this time and think, *I spent too much time with her.*" I agreed. "If you're going to go...commit. Don't go half-in," I felt like a star player getting a locker room pep talk. I hate sports.

I went. It was a December evening. Half the group showed up late. Of course they did. *These woo-shit ding-dongs can channel galactic energies, but can't arrive on time?* I was judging. Hard. If you really had the power of the universe at your fingertips, why couldn't you get it together?

When the facilitator went around the circle and asked how excited we were to be there, women I'd never met called out "Eight!," "Ten!," "Twelve!." When it got to me, I said, flatly, "One-point-five. And I'm ready to run."

I meant it.

I could say that night changed my life—but really, it didn't. The *cancer* changed my life. That night, simply removed the armor. It made it possible for me to be present. This circle of strangers, both known and unknown entered into a realm where we didn't need to know. A little plant took my hand, and through the doors of a meditation, walked me into the chamber of my heart.

I laid down my sword while I held my sorrow. I held her that night. We'd been best friends for decades, and I'd never held her. Not once. Our hugs were polite, shoulder-to-shoulder, quick exits. Too much exposure was dangerous—too painful. Too tender.

But that night, we held each other. Fully.

My fear shut off like a switch and my heart unfurled like a sail untethered for the first time—flapping wildly, overflowing, unproductive.

It didn't fix anything. It didn't cure her. But it opened something.

And when I got home, I held my children. Not just a hug. I *held* them.

Of course, I had held them before—nursed them, soothed them, loved them—but I had never really held them. Not like this. And when I didn't let go, they didn't let go either. I hadn't known they needed that. But they did. And so did I.

I began to understand: tenderness is not weakness. Humility is not self-loathing. And the *woo*?

It was just love.

Raw, untidy, electrifying love.

And we *all* have access to it.

Our entire family changed. We slowed down. We opened up. We became a family of connection—still chaotic, still imperfect —but full of love. I can be touched now. By my husband. By my friends.

We held her memorial on the same day as my daughter's birthday party.

The very daughter she had helped me bring into the world. She'd been there in the labor room, witnessing, *presence-ing*. It was a Barbie party. A bright, pink, joyful Barbie party that ended and then transitioned into Kris's "celebration of life."

I didn't know what to make of it.

Grief is bizarre. You read that it comes in waves—and it does. One day, you're crying your eyes out for hours, and the next you feel completely dried out, emotionless for days. You wonder if you *should* be crying. You wonder why you *can't* cry. You feel guilty for laughing.

When you have to tell people what's going on, you question whether you're expected to burst into tears—or if that would just make everyone uncomfortable. How do you make the *exact right face*—the one that doesn't offload your discomfort, but still shows you're in a fair amount of distress?

Do I look soft enough?

Do I look too happy?

If I smile, am I negating the pain?

I've never thought about my face so much.

We invited all of the "woo crew"—the people who had surrounded her as she was dying, clinging to the last drops of her magic as she evaporated. I knew some of them, but not all. It was perhaps the first time all the containers—those carefully orchestrated circles, pockets, modules of her life—were gathered in one place. Spread out at a barbecue for us all to see, we met each other, most of us for the first time.

Stories were exchanged. Myths. Labels. We were discovering how we had been positioned: what kind of friends we were, how we were described, how we were connected—and how we had been kept apart. Each of us had seen only a fragment of her, never the whole.

"I am my phenomenal absence," wrote Wei Wu Wei.

And she was.

Phenomenal.

Absent and present.

Everywhere, and only in parts.

We ate Korean barbecue and princess cake. We drank white wine and told stories. Toward the end of the evening, some of the woo crew snuggled on the couch, cuddling, holding each other—desperate for connection.

I sat in *our* spot on the couch, the one where she and I used to sit, doing what I can only describe as complaining. I complained about the containers, the compartmentalization. I wondered: *Who am I with right now? Which version are you?*

I was mad at my friend.

As I complained about her—about the parade, the stories, the red lipstick, the fake tits. And then—mid-rant—one of the paper lanterns hanging from the ceiling snapped off its string and smacked me directly on the head.

Everyone gasped.

She was obviously there. And she did *not* like what I was saying. The woo was strong with this one.

But that moment—ridiculous as it was—also marked the beginning of a slow and subtle shift. A softening. A loosening of something rigid in me. At the time, I laughed it off. But I think she was already pulling me toward something.

A repair.

This compartmentalization that had so angered me at her ~~funeral~~, *celebration of life*, was her means of survival, but she didn't survive. It didn't work. The knock to the head was less of a "shut up" and more of a "wake up." She was knocking me upside the head through the echoes.

Months passed. Maybe a year. Life rearranged itself in the way it does after a loss—quietly, disjointedly. The world kept turning. My children kept growing. Her absence kept shape-shifting.

Then one day, I stood in front of my bathroom mirror, and she was there. I froze...terrified she would disappear.

I can't explain how. I don't need to.

But she was there.

Shining in a golden smock, a turquoise jewel at her throat. Not metaphorically. Not imaginatively. *Present*. Shimmering in that way the spirit world shows itself—just on the edge of knowing. Whatever we were seeing, we were seeing it together—her on her side, me on mine. We were sisters. We were the makers of planets. We had stardust running through our veins. We were the makers of magic, and it was all around us. It's all around *all* of us.

There we stood, facing the mirror—she on her side, me on mine. We locked eyes through a veil as thin as glass—transparent, delicate. In that moment, it was as if we were both being seen, both unveiled at once.

I had always imagined that when she crossed over, everything would become clear to her, all things revealed. But what took me by surprise was that it wasn't just her clarity—it was ours. Together, we witnessed the unfolding. And it truly was an unfolding, a revelation we could never access when she was alive.

We saw each other as we really were. Not just best friends, but mirrors. Not soulmates or sisters in another life, necessarily— but women bound by something old and unspoken. Something that transcended this one lifetime without needing to define its origins. We loved each other. And yet, there had always been tension.

She was grace. I was grit.

She was mystery. I was voice.

Together, we were unlike anything in this world. We were massive. We were powerful.

We each resented the other's gifts at times, secretly coveting what we didn't feel we could embody ourselves. There was envy, sure—but the love ran deeper still.

In the mirror, it was clear: the only way forward was to mend the bond.

Not just for her, or for me—but for *us*.

The distance, the push-pull, the old competition—it had all brought us here. To the wound. To the source. To the place we hadn't been brave enough to enter together until now.

We hadn't always managed to work together in life. But now, on the other side of everything, our work was just beginning.

She was still urging me toward something. Whispering to the living: *You don't have to go all the way to cancer to wake up.* You don't have to die to heal your family. You don't have to wait until the end to love fully.

I was pulled back to that last time I was in her bedroom, lying on her bed–connecting the threads.

I was pulled back to her visions. She was on stage, speaking. "It doesn't have to be this way. Life can be full of love. Of growth. Of magic."

She saw herself in a white suit. White hair. Blazing red lipstick. A shocking image, she said. Then she looked at me and said, *"Pick up the pen."*

I told her I would. I'll write this for her. For us. This was *Catcher in the Rye* shit. *You don't have to go all the way to cancer to wake up.* "Tell as many of them as you can," she said.

Here she was in this mirror in another striking image–always with the parade. But the parade changed for me then. I understood. I got onto the great elephant in the room with her and walked it into the light–right into the center ring.

That's when I realized...we all *want* to talk about the elephant. We're desperate to talk about the elephant. We don't know how. She didn't know how. So, I invite you to take my hand and climb up on this great elephant with me. We'll make friends with the behemoth.

Now I see her everywhere and nowhere. She is her phenomenal absence–but also her presence. She is just right there, always. She won't stand on that stage alone. I'll stand on that stage...with her. Maybe I'll tell this story. And if I do, maybe I'll see her in the crowd—white hair, red lips, dark skin, white suit—and I'll know it's her.

Will we be complete?

No.

We'll just be getting started.

MELISSA MCCANN-TILTON

Melissa McCann-Tilton is a revenue strategist, organizational futurist, and unapologetic truth-teller on a mission to rewrite the rules of work—and the inner lives of those doing it. As President and Chief Revenue Officer at Criteria Corp, she drives growth with humanity, blending strategic firepower with grounded presence.

She's led companies through hypergrowth, high-stakes exits, and the occasional spectacular implosion—earning a battle-tested understanding of what it means to build, break, and rebuild with intention.

Raised in religious extremism in the Deep South, Melissa once used business as armor. But everything changed in 2023, when the loss of her best friend sparked a spiritual reckoning. Grief became an initiation—into stillness, surrender, and the deeper truths she'd outrun through success.

A mother of four and conscious growth advocate, Melissa invites you to dismantle what no longer serves and build something more alive, aligned, and human.

https://www.linkedin.com/in/mccanntilton/
https://www.instagram.com/melissamccanntilton/
https://www.facebook.com/mccanntilton

2

WHOSE BODY IS THIS

BY JO ALBERTSON

At a time when other three-year-olds were learning shapes, colors, and words, I was having a spiritual awakening.

It was a crisp, cool day in October, and I was playing outside with two of my girlfriends. Our house was on the corner, one side faced our street, and the other side faced the main street that took you in and out of town. I adored animals, and across the main street lived a beautiful Collie named Lady. Sometimes when her owner walked her down our street, I would rush over to pet her. Lady was a friendly dog and always welcomed my attention. She would run up to me, wagging her tail in anticipation of me petting her and talking to her.

One day, Lady was alone in her yard, and she looked lonely. When we saw her, we all ran across the main street to play with her, not seeing the car speeding down the hill. My friends made it across, just as the car flew past them. But I was not so lucky, before I knew it, I was flying in the air. The car hit me with such force that my body went flying in the air, landing with the loudest thump!

Tires screeching and children screaming got the attention of the telephone man up on the pole, and my mother, who was in the basement ironing. The man made it to me first and started CPR. I wasn't breathing! When I regained consciousness, the first thing I saw was my mother. She looked terrified. When the ambulance arrived, I said to my mother, "Mommy, I can't feel my leg."

My leg was broken, with the bone sticking out. Once at the hospital, it wasn't long before I slowly drifted into a coma due to the brain swelling from the concussion. They determined I had a compound fracture in my leg, a broken arm, and a fractured skull. We did not have the medical advances that we have now, so they waited to put casts on my broken bones just in case I didn't make it. I was in a coma for three days. It was during that time that I took a journey.

Each person who has a near-death experience tells their story based on their beliefs, religion, and understanding of their world. I was three, which makes my story a little different than most, and yet common with everyone who has had this occur in their life.

When I arrived across the veil, I found myself in a large room, similar to a train station, full of activity with people moving in every direction. Some were going up like on an escalator, but there wasn't a physical structure. Their bodies were airborne as they floated upward. Everyone had an escort or two, someone who was assisting them to get to where they needed to be. It was joyful. People were laughing and talking, but it wasn't in a language of words; it sounded like tones, vibrations, and music, and everyone knew the language. I even understood what they were saying. It looked chaotic, but it wasn't. It was peaceful, filled with a love that I had never felt before. What I found most interesting was the loving feeling and how it was expressed to everyone and everything.

I was sitting at a wooden picnic table off to the side of most of the activity, with a coloring book and crayons. There was a man sitting next to me. He had such kind eyes and a gentle smile. His face was round, his eyes were blue, and he had a full head of hair. Not too heavy, but not too thin, and I didn't get the impression he was tall. I felt like I knew him, but I didn't recognize his face. He spoke softly to me, which made me feel comfortable; I wasn't afraid.

I questioned the man, "Where are the people going on the escalator?"

He spoke softly and said, "Heaven."

"What about the other people?" I whispered.

He told me, "They are being taken to different places before they go up the escalator. Most of them have just arrived, just like you."

About that time, a brilliant, bright light came and asked me to follow it, so I did. There was no face, only the tallest, brightest light I had ever seen. It had three light beings next to it that I began referring to as my three friends. One was taller than the others, one was very round, and the third was a normal shape. They didn't have bodies, but rather white glowing lights. They were not the brilliant white light like the tall being, but rather a softer, gentler hue. We went into a room like a movie theatre with a big screen. There, the light showed me picture after picture of what I was destined to do and many ways to do it. All the pictures were of the human body, sometimes the whole body, and sometimes only parts of the body. I was fascinated by how it all went together. The light would show me every angle you could imagine. First, it showed a body part by itself, then the whole body, then another part, and put it all together again. The light being repeated these images multiple times, so I could see how the body worked.

I remember thinking, *I can do that. That looks like fun!* And just as fast as the pictures were being shown to me...*poof*, I was suddenly back in my body.

While I was away, my body was fighting hard to stay alive. Some of my body went into shock and some of my organs were not functioning properly. When I woke up, my three light friends were there with my mom and dad. The day finally came to get the cast put on my broken leg and arm. As they took me into a dark, eerie room, I screamed for my mother. Terrified of the dark, I saw my mother's worried face staring at me from the door.

When I was released from the hospital, cast and all, my parents had to keep me in a dark room for a while until the concussion symptoms disappeared. Knowing that I was afraid of the dark, my sister would sneak in to play with me. Of course, she got in a lot of trouble if she got caught, but it was very comforting for me. I still had my three friends with me. They would make me laugh by zooming all around the room, doing circles. I could hear them laughing, and that made me laugh too. They told me that being in the dark wasn't scary, that it could be fun too. They spoke in the same language I heard when I was in the big room, sitting at the picnic table. I could tell them apart because each had a different tone when they spoke. Teaching me about the darkness was one of the many things they would show me.

My mother was on her own spiritual quest that began in her childhood, always questioning things. So, when I asked questions or told her what I was seeing or feeling, she did not ridicule me, make it shameful, or tell me I was just making it up. I played with my three spirit friends, I talked with them, and I learned from them. They talked to me about my body and how I got hurt, and how I was healing. They would show me snapshots of what I saw in the room about bodies to remind me. The most intriguing image was the spider network that was all over the body. Later, I would learn that it was our energy field, but as a three-year-old, I would try and touch it. When we played outside, they showed me the spider network and how it was everywhere and connected to everything. Their tones would be higher-pitched when they got excited, and the vibrations would get stronger. We played a lot of games, which is how they taught me about the body, the music, vibrations, and tones of the cells. I enjoyed their company.

One day, my mother explained to me that these friends would soon be gone because they would have to go help another boy or girl who got hurt like me. I was so thankful she did that because when they did leave, I knew someone else needed them.

Some people would argue that a young child does not have the mental capabilities to understand the magnitude of a near-death experience. I beg to differ. Children come into this world innocent, full of love and compassion for all living beings. An understanding that they came from the divine. (For clarification of the meaning of "divine for this chapter, it means "something beyond the ordinary, something that inspires awe, reverence, and a sense of connection to something greater than oneself.") Children have an innate sense of right or wrong, good or bad. Just because they do not have command of their language verbally does not mean they do not have command of the language of their heart. I understood exactly what my three spirit friends showed me, the connections to all living things, which included everything on Earth.

Throughout my childhood, I played with toys that taught me parts of the body, like Mr. Potato Head. It was extremely interesting how the body worked, all bodies. I spent hours outside observing nature, talking with everything and anything that would listen. I would ask the trees what they saw from their limbs and ask the ants about the houses they had under the ground. I found nature to be my solace. When I was on the other side, sitting at the picnic table, the whole room was filled with such love and compassion. Everything there had such beauty; the colors were brighter, the fragrances were different, and everything vibrated and sounded like music. It was so peaceful. After my accident, I was always asking my mother why people were so mean, why they did not act like what I saw on the other side, and why they couldn't remember what it was like to be over there! It was frustrating to me; I spent my younger years searching every place I encountered to see if maybe this was the place on Earth where I would find those feelings, but I never did. Nature, the animals, and water were the closest places I could find.

My mother did a fabulous job explaining our world to me so that I could cope. When I was younger, she explained to me that everyone on the planet has a gift; some discover theirs, and some do not. Mine was being empathic and the ability to sense a vibrational message from living things. My three spirit friends showed me how to feel, hear, and understand some of the meanings within the spider web. Fast-forward years after the accident, my mother became my first spiritual mentor, my biology, anatomy, and psychology coach, which assisted me with the destiny I was given at three years old. She was studying to be a nutritional consultant and had all kinds of books that she shared with me. This started when I was twelve and continued until I graduated with my Master's Degree. I was determined to fulfill the promise I made to that bright light that I would do the work and help make our world a better place by helping others.

In my studies with my mother, we discussed at length that human beings are energy first and physical second. This conversation started when I was young. I asked her about the spider web that I could feel but not see. I was in kindergarten when I started humming a tune, repeating the same sounds as my mother listened.

Finally, she said, "Jo, what are you humming?"

I told her, "It's the song of the spider web."

She knew about the spider web, so she asked, "Whose spider web?"

I told her it was my teacher's. When the bright light was showing me all the pictures, it showed me that all bodies have a song, a vibration that is uniquely their own. Even though my three spirit friends had gone away, I could still hear them talking in my head.

I mentioned it to my mom, and she said, "Oh, Jo, those are your spirit guides; everyone has at least one, and some have more." I asked her if they were my three spirit friends, and she said, "No, those friends had a different job to do; these will be with you your entire life."

My first memory of reading a body was when I was either seven or eight years old. We had a dachshund named Schmitty. He was doing zoomies across the living room when we heard a yipe! My mom ran in to see what was wrong, and he couldn't move his back legs. She immediately put him under an infrared light focused on his low back. Mom did this for several days, but he still wasn't using his back legs. One day, I was lying on the floor with him while he was under the light. I started to pet him and ran my hands down his spine. Suddenly, I ran into a bone that was out of place.

I could hear in my head, *touch the muscles on either side and rub up and down,* so I did. I don't know if the voice was Schmitty's or my guides, but I followed the instructions and did that several times that day. It wasn't long before he was running around doing his zoomies.

I was learning at a young age to trust my guides and my intuition, playing with the energy field with my hands and body. I was nine years old, my parents had hosted the block bridge game, and my mom let me stay up late.

I was helping her clean up the tables, and I said to her, "Mrs. Browning really likes Mr. Reynolds."

My mother replied, "Oh course, we are neighbors."

I repeated what I said again.

My mother, getting a little perturbed, said, "Yes, Jo, I know we are all good friends."

To which I replied, "No, they like each other like you and Daddy do."

That caught my mother's attention quickly! We found out later they were having an affair, but how did a nine-year-old know that? Because the energy was so strong, and that was the only way I could express it.

Mom and I discussed the spider-web a lot while I was young, and it merged into discussions about the magnetic energy field around everything. Some people just call it *the field*. One day, I walked into a room after a heated argument.

The energy was so thick I thought, *Wow, you could cut that with a knife.*

Cut what? It's the energy I walked into.

We are sending and receiving information constantly during the day and while we sleep. Every thought that has ever been thought lies within this field. I had a friend who was going to write a book, but before she could complete it, someone else wrote one just like it. Why? The idea was in the field, and someone received it and acted on it.

When I was in high school, I knew I wanted to have my own business and had no intention of going to college. Thanks to my father's friend who told me, "Well, if you want people to take you seriously, you need a degree."

That statement changed my entire life. I majored in Physical Education and Health because that would give me the science and psychology of the human body. After graduation, I was a permanent substitute at my high school and became the JV basketball coach.

As a little girl, my favorite shows were about cowboys and cowgirls. I loved the adventures, the horses, and the scenery. I had a yearning to be in the Wild West. When I got older, my mother told me that when I was 4 years old, I told her I wanted to go home. My mother pulled out a map of the United States, and she pointed to Illinois and told me that it was my home. She said I took my little finger and pointed to Texas and said, "I want to go home!"

After finishing my master's degree, I moved to Dallas with no job and no friends, just a strong desire to move HOME. I convinced an apartment complex to lease an apartment to me, even though I didn't have a job, and off I went I worked for major corporations, Revlon, Merck, and Ross Laboratories, gathering skills that would assist me in owning my own company.

In 1984, I opened Massage Consultants in Dallas, Texas. I had a business partner and two therapists. We were in the headquarters of a nationwide restaurant chain that supplied us with four therapy rooms and a 300-square-foot office. There were 350 employees in this building, and we provided stress management chair massages and full-body massages. We also provided massage therapy for the medical and psychological community. There are many modalities of massage therapy; we chose deep-tissue, sports massage, Swedish, Reiki, prenatal, and cranio-sacral. Each one of us had our specialty, mine was the Body-Mind connection using Swedish, Reiki, and Cranio-Sacral.

When I completed my massage therapy training, I created a marketing campaign for physicians, psychologists, psychiatrists, and counselors explaining the body-mind connections and cellular memory for healing. At this time, the concept of the body-mind connection was still very new, and very few healthcare practitioners knew about cellular memory. To explain cellular memory, think of your body as a walking encyclopedia of your life. Within the cells of the body are stored memories of information, events, and exposures to the external world. This storage of information is in cells outside of the brain.

My business with the body-mind connection took off like wildfire as the counseling industry saw the value, as well as the physicians. I started doing my own case studies to validate things I saw in my practice. I asked my clients questions: where were you born, how many siblings do you have, what is your birth date? All this information formulated how they would relate to their body. There were reasons people disassociated from their bodies, most centered around some sort of trauma. It was the mid-1980s, and prior to the acronym of PTSD, we just called it trauma. One of the psychiatrists I worked with called me and told me about a patient, and she felt they were stuck, but wasn't sure why. Her patient set up an appointment to see if I could uncover anything. A petite woman arrived at my office. She wore a business suit, a starched shirt, pantyhose, and heels. A quiet woman, she was an accountant for a major firm in town, and you could tell she kept to herself. She told me she was concerned because she kept losing time and didn't know why. The massage started like any other, soft soothing music, the room was dim with lighting, and no one was talking. Suddenly, the energy shifted in the room; her once soft, subtle muscles became harder and more restricted.

A deep voice says, "Is that all you're going to do?"

Startled, I looked up toward the lady's head to see who had just spoken, and to my shock, the sheet was pulled halfway down to her waist, exposing her breasts. I quickly covered her up and gazed into her eyes, but they were different- more seductive.

She repeated herself, "Is this all you're going to do?"

"Yes, this is a therapeutic massage, not a sexual massage," I replied.

"How unfortunate," she replied.

One of the things I learned from my three spirit friends regarding the energy field is that it changes based on thoughts, emotions, or observations from the person. This small, quiet, petite woman was engulfed with sexual energy and a boldness she did not have when we met. I asked this person who she was and received an entirely different name. She told me she was responsible for the gaps in time that this client could not remember. That my client was boring, and it was her job to help her have some fun.

"How many others are there?" I asked her.

She spoke softly as she described each and every one who lived within this small frame. This personality told me there might be others, but she didn't know for sure. I told this person she would have to leave because the session was over, and to bring back my client. When the lady opened her eyes, she knew immediately that she had lost time. I told her I would call her psychiatrist right after the session and tell her what happened. I also suggested she call the doctor and set up an appointment right away so the doctor could explain what had happened. I never saw this woman again, but heard later that she eventually consolidated all her personalities and went on to live a joyous life.

Humans are not the only ones that possess the ability to read energy; so do animals. I had a Dalmatian named Moire (pronounced more-ray). I started taking her to work with me. We had a magical relationship, very telepathic. One day, a new client came to see me, one sent by a counselor. The lady had been severely abused for years. She couldn't stand to have anyone close to her, let alone touch her. I wasn't quite sure how to start the process of getting her back into her body, but I knew something would show up! And it sure did...Moire.

The woman entered my office terrified. I asked her to sit on the couch, and I sat across from her in a chair, at a distance that she was comfortable with. She was closed off, muscles tight, void of expression in her face.

"I don't know why I'm here. I can't stand to have anyone touch me," She said,

"That's okay," I told her. "Let's start by talking about how you feel about your body."

About that time, Moire came around the corner and stopped. She looked at me and then looked at the client. Slowly, she approached this woman. Moire got right up next to her, turned around, and sat down so her back was facing her. The woman lit up when Moire walked into the room. She started petting the dog and telling me her story through her tears. As the sessions progressed, Moire would look at the woman's body in certain areas, look back at me as if to say, *Do you see there's no energy here*, and she was always correct. It was a magical experience working with Moire, and we continued with many more clients. This client eventually, after over six months, finally received a massage and liked it!

My mother told me when I was young that in our world, anything is possible, and I believed her. She taught me that if you are going to listen to your inner intelligence, you have to get quiet and clear your mind. As I progressed in the field of energy healing and bodywork, I took classes, studied with people who were excelling in the field, and absorbed as much information as I could. Before each session I have with a client, I quiet my mind, ask my guides and the guides of my client to show me how I can help. It feels like a vacuum, no thoughts of mine, and I wait. I wait for the vibrations, emotions, and the sounds of the body, and then the conversation begins. It could be a current topic or a past trauma; it has both joys of life and hardships. I listen, and I am guided to the part of the body that needs help. Our bodies are very intelligent, far more than we have been taught. I saw this in the cinema room on the other side of the veil and have witnessed thousands of sessions that confirm this knowledge.

Each person has their own unique vibration, and while it may take time to hear and understand the language of the body, anyone can do it. We are all mystical, magical beings, and it is my deepest hope that we can all experience the fullness of who we are.

JO ALBERTSON

Since 1986, as a healthcare practitioner, Jo has developed the ability to help her clients understand the science behind their body-mind connection as well as a spiritual understanding behind their soul's journey. It's amazing what life can be like when the body, mind and spirit work together in synchrony.

Jo's mission is to help people learn to listen to and trust the divine and ever-present voice inside that is ready to offer guidance, comfort and inspiration at any time. Jo has both a bachelor's and master's degree in physical education and health. She was a licensed Massage Therapist, a Massage Therapy Instructor, and is a certified Reiki III practitioner. When you love yourself enough to look within, you truly do become your own best friend.

Website: www.joalbertson.com
Facebook: https://www.facebook.com/jo.albertson.7

3

MIND GAMES

BY CHRISTY JAYNES

At twenty-two, I was brimming with the kind of audacity that only youth can provide—the belief that anything was possible, even if I didn't know exactly how. I was wandering the world of self-help, eager to explore the tools that could shape my destiny. That's when I discovered Shakti Gawain's *Creative Visualization*. I read it like it held the secrets of the universe, and in many ways, it did. Her words became my guide. I didn't wait for permission or perfect conditions. I simply jumped in and began visualizing—first small things, then bigger ones.

At first, the results were subtle. A parking space when I needed one. A small check in the mail when money was tight. Over time, I realized that these weren't coincidences; they were the results of my thoughts and intentions becoming reality. It was like discovering a hidden superpower, I can hone through belief and practice.

I started a journal, an innocent little book where I could dream and wish, a container for all the things I wanted. I made lists, detailing everything from material desires to abstract dreams. I clipped pictures from magazines and catalogs: shoes, watches, homes—things I desired, each image a silent promise. I pasted them in the pages, organizing them like a vision board that I could return to at will. But life moved on, and I forgot about it. The journal slipped from my mind, left forgotten in the chaos of everyday life.

A year passed.

Then, as I was preparing for a move across town, I stumbled across the book while sorting through a box from the top of my closet. I'm highly distractible and sat down to flip through the pages, half-expecting to find a relic of old wishes, nothing more. But what I saw stunned me. The watch I had clipped a picture of was on my wrist. The shoes I had wanted? There they were, neatly tucked into my closet. And the house I had so vividly imagined? I was about to step over its threshold, ready to move in.

I sat there, stunned, as I continued flipping through the pages. More than half of the things I had listed, things I had long since forgotten about, had already come to fruition. It wasn't just wishful thinking; it was proof that the universe had been quietly aligning itself with the intentions I had set, even when I wasn't paying attention. The journal, the lists, the pictures, they weren't just dreams on paper. They were stepping stones, gently guiding me toward a reality I hadn't fully realized I was creating.

Around the same time, I watched a PBS special by Deepak Chopra. His words about self-healing through visualization felt authentic to me, although I'd never really heard of anything like it before. He guided viewers through a visualization where they imagine themselves lying in a stream of healing water, a grid forming over their body. The water would fill each square, washing away disease, dark energy, and any blockages, leaving you whole and vibrant. I was captivated. It felt like the universe was handing me another key to unlock deeper, more profound healing.

Just a short while later, life gave me a test I wasn't expecting.

I was in a terrible car accident that sent me to the intensive care unit. I could feel the rushing of blood down my thigh as the ER nurses cut my clothes off my body. "Look at my thigh, look at my thigh," I cried, my own eyes crusted shut with blood. But there was nothing to see, except a bruise the size of a dinner plate over my hip. As I lay on a metal table in a dark room, waiting for the doctors to bring in the X-ray machine, I remembered that visualization. The one I had learned from Chopra. And in that moment, I knew I had a choice.

Instead of succumbing to the fear and pain surrounding me, I felt calm—thoughtful, even—and in that moment, I chose to visualize. I imagined that healing stream of water flowing over me, the grid covering my body, each square being washed clean. I didn't know if it would work, but I trusted the process. And when they were done picking all of the glass bits from my body, I was released.

When I left the hospital, my body was covered in cuts, bruises, and a black eye. It was hard to believe anything had shifted in those first few hours. I stayed at my parents' house, healing on the sofa overnight and the next day. I worked for a company that would not believe me if I called and said I had been in a terrible car accident. So, I borrowed my mom's car and drove down to work. One of my bosses met me outside. He took one look and, with empathy and deep concern in his eyes, sent me home to heal. But two days later, something extraordinary happened. My bruises were fading, my energy was returning, and the cuts

—well, they were healing at a rate that defied all logic. I looked almost normal. And the pain? It had diminished significantly. When I showed back up at work, my other boss proclaimed that I had been faking because I "looked fine." But the manager who had sent me home spoke up, saying, "No, I saw her; she was in terrible shape." Then he turned to me and asked, "How did you heal so fast?"

"Visualization," I replied over my shoulder as I walked back to my office.

This wasn't a miracle in the traditional sense, but to me, it felt like one.

This experience wasn't just about healing my body; it was about learning to trust the unseen forces that guide us. My intuition, which had been whispering through all the years before this moment, suddenly became a booming voice. The more I listened, the more I realized that intuition was my greatest superpower. The key to unlocking a life of miracles wasn't about forcing outcomes; it was about learning to master my mind, to align with universal energy, and to act on the knowing that was already inside me.

What some dismiss as "woo-woo," I recognize as an intrinsic way of life, a way of engaging with the world that transcends conventional understanding. When people label something as woo-woo, I see it as an expression of their inability to grasp the depth of what's happening, an easy way to categorize the unknown. It's like calling someone "artsy" or "crafty" without truly seeing the artistry or craftsmanship at work. They may say, "They're good at making things, but I don't really understand what they're doing; it's just craft." Yet the person being judged is creating from a place of profound skill and refinement. The observer simply cannot perceive the depth of it. In my experience, what's often labeled as woo-woo is rooted in a deep, intuitive wisdom drawn from the vast stream of collective consciousness. A knowledge that, though invisible, is as real and powerful as any other form of knowing. I didn't always understand things this way, but I have always been willing to examine new ideas.

I've used that same creative visualization process for countless things in my life, whether it was healing, manifesting opportunities, or simply creating peace in moments of chaos. The results were never instant, and the path wasn't always linear, but the more I trusted the process, the more the universe responded in kind. It's the difference between waiting for something magical to happen, and engaging directly with the universal intelligence that is waiting for us to direct it with our thoughts and actions.

Before I ever encountered Deepak Chopra or his teachings, I had my own inner wisdom—a knowing that stretched beyond what I was taught. As a teenager, I was told by my dentist that my wisdom teeth were growing downward, burrowing into the roots of my molars. She explained that I would need oral surgery to extract the impacted teeth, a procedure I had no desire to endure. Instead of accepting that fate, I decided to take matters into my own hands quietly, but with fierce intention. I began visualizing my teeth shifting, imagining them turning upwards, breaking through my gums as they should, just like regular teeth.

Months passed.

Then, one day, it happened. My teeth did precisely what I had visualized. A new set of molars appeared in the back of my mouth. When I returned to the dentist for a follow-up, she was puzzled. Her X-rays showed something entirely unexplainable;

my wisdom teeth had corrected themselves. She reviewed the images again, furrowing her brow, clearly confused. I could feel the grin spreading across my face as I cheerfully explained, "I visualized my teeth fixing themselves, and they did."

She stared at me, her expression a mix of disbelief and professional skepticism. "That is not a thing that happens," she said curtly, dismissing my claims as if they were no more than the musings of a teenager. But as she hovered over my chair, the silence between us thickened. She studied me, almost as if she were trying to decipher a puzzle she couldn't quite solve. The evidence was there, clear as day, but her mind could not reconcile what her eyes had seen. That moment was a quiet turning point for me, a confirmation that the power of the mind was more real than I had ever known.

An understanding took hold of me sometime in the last fifty years, although I cannot tell you the day, month, or year. My clarity about how my connection to the universe has become so evident through what some may term coincidences, serendipity, woo-woo, or luck. To put it simply: so many amazing things happen to me that are made to order and cannot be explained, that I have no choice but to pay attention and seek more understanding. My thoughts are the current that flows between us, me and all there is. How I think is what I experience. I want to heal, and so I do. I want my teeth to straighten up, and they do. I want all kinds of "things", objects that delight me, and eventually they come. But I am careless with my power. I often forget how powerful I can be. I don't remember to use it for good and not as a detriment to myself, for my negative thoughts are just as powerful as my positive or creative thoughts. The universe is always listening, and I am always transmitting. In this life, I will dance until my dying day, and some days that feels like it will be sooner than later.

In 2015, I was brutally assaulted by a man high on drugs, an experience that shattered me in ways I couldn't fully comprehend at the time. The physical damage to my body took years to heal, but it was my soul that endured the most prolonged recovery. Trauma penetrates every part of us, leaving invisible scars that resurface in every quiet moment. In the immediate aftermath, I found a small solace in the act of visualization. I began imagining myself living at a convent, somewhere far from the world, where I could spend my days tending to a garden and serving others in peace. Every time despair crept in, every time I wanted to give up on my life, I would return to this vision. It was a retreat, a mental sanctuary that brought me fleeting moments of calm.

A year later, my life had taken an unexpected turn. I found myself in a caregiving role for my future mother-in-law, a role I had never asked for, living in a small bedroom with my belongings packed away in a storage unit. I spent my days cooking, cleaning, and eventually gardening; activities I had never imagined for myself at this stage of life. This wasn't the future I had envisioned for my middle-aged years... or was it?

One day, as I worked in the garden I had created from a barren gravel patch, something shifted inside me. The realization hit me with a quiet force: I was living the life I had imagined. It wasn't a convent, of course, because it wasn't practical, nor was it aligned with my life as a mother and partner. But the essence of that vision, the simplicity, the service, the grounding in nature, was here in this small corner of the world I had not chosen but was now embracing. I was living a life of service, tending to the land, and learning patience and reverence for a person who had lost so many memories, but was still a whole being.

Tears welled in my eyes as I recognized the miracle that had unfolded. The universe had given me exactly what I needed, just not in the way I had expected. My heart swelled with gratitude as I understood the profound way in which this experience came to me. It wasn't an accident; it was the life I had visualized, appearing in a form that aligned with my current reality.

From that day forward, caregiving took on new meaning. It wasn't just an obligation, it was a calling, a chance to give in ways I hadn't imagined. But more than that, it became a part of my healing process. Through the act of giving and serving, I began to reclaim myself. I set new goals: to heal fully, to become a whole woman again, one who could engage with the world comfortably, with love and purpose, instead of fear and pain.

There's an old saying, *pearls before swine,* which I often use to describe people who cannot grasp the nuanced beauty or depth of something. It's a way of illustrating how certain experiences, ideas, or truths can be lost on those who aren't attuned to them. But, more often than I'd like to admit, I am the swine. I look at aspects of my life and feel dissatisfied, convinced that something is missing, that my circumstances aren't as they should be. It's only when I shift my perspective that I realize what I've been given is exactly what I need. It simply hasn't arrived in the form I expected.

In those moments, I realized that I didn't have the eyes to see or the ears to hear. I hadn't fully opened my heart and mind to the truth that I am not just a passive observer in my life, I am its co-creator. When I do open myself to this possibility, I begin to see evidence of it everywhere. The pieces of my life fall into place, not as random events, but as parts of a bigger picture I helped shape. It becomes clear that I have the power to choose. I can look at the miracles right in front of me, choose to believe in their significance, and embrace their wisdom, or I can turn away from them, dismissing their truth. Just like my dentist, I stand at the crossroads of perception: to see or not to see. And when I choose to see, I witness the miracles that have always been there, waiting for me to recognize them.

I'm not here to offer a step-by-step guide to manifesting miracles. I do want to share an understanding that the mind holds tremendous power to heal, to create, and to shape reality. It's about tuning into that quiet voice inside that knows what you need and acting on it, no matter how audacious it may seem.

In this life, when we choose to engage with the energy of the universe, it responds. It's not always about seeing things with our eyes, but about knowing that, in the unseen, everything we need is already there. The key is listening. The key is trusting. The key is to remember that miracles are not just for the lucky few; they are for all of us, if we are brave enough to embrace them.

CHRISTY JAYNES

Christy is a seasoned branding coach and storyteller who has spent decades exploring the profound connection between mind, spirit, and healing. With a passion for creative visualization and intuitive wisdom, she guides others to unlock their inner power and manifest lives filled with purpose and possibility. Drawing from personal experience and a deep well of insight, Christy invites readers to embrace the miracles that arise when we learn to master our minds and trust the unseen flow of universal energy.

Her current projects include a new book release in the fall of 2025 called *From The Ground Up*, an invitation to and an argument for women stepping into civic leadership. Her agency, Electa, serves women running for office by creating a candidate brand and message, materials, and media that will help them rise above the noise and capture the attention of voters.

Website: www.electaagency.com
Instagram: https://www.instagram.com/electa.agency

4

FROM BOO TO WOO

BY MICHELLE SAVAGE

They say you'll always remember your first, so you'd think I could remember the first time I was haunted. But after five years of regular sightings, the lady-ghost that came with our hundred-year-old Victorian house became as integrated into my memories as the family dog - just part of the gang.

She wore a long, white dress with a high ruffly collar and covered buttons running down the front – an outfit suggesting that unless she croaked at a retro costume party, she'd been there from the beginning. Long black hair fell loose around her face, and I would say she was tall for a woman of her time, but it's difficult to estimate someone's height when they're floating above you. Like standing on your tippy toes at the doctor's office, it feels like a cheat.

One night, when I was lying in bed in the dark with my bedroom door open, I watched her glide up the stairs and cross the landing to my big sister's room. Initially, I was relieved that my sister had been chosen as the night's lucky hauntee. We'd been taught to take turns, and this time it was hers. But moments later, I felt the ghost's presence moving toward my room, ready to defile my good night's sleep with her sloppy seconds of terror.

I pulled the blankets tight under my chin, squeezed my eyes shut, and waited. A short moment later, my bed frame rocked beneath me, like she was nudging me awake with her foot. Opening my eyes, I was transfixed by her expressionless gaze. She neither looked evil nor like she'd be much fun at parties. With a mysterious weight pressing on my chest, I couldn't breathe or talk or call out for help; it felt like she'd sucked the air out of my lungs. I didn't dare to blink or look away, afraid of what she might do if I moved so much as a muscle. But when my eyes began to water and burn, I closed them again. When I finally dared to peek, she was gone.

Lady-ghost was not the only supernatural inhabitant in that old house, but she's the only one I can personally recall. My mother tells a story about me playing in our unfinished basement and then promptly reporting that there was a man downstairs by the furnace. Perhaps it's strange that I refer to the ghosts in our house as *my* ghosts, the way one refers to *my* hairstylist or *my* mechanic, as if the relationship was optional or to my benefit. It's not like Lady-ghost showed up at regular intervals to give me a trim or a tune-up. She popped in just enough to keep me petrified of the dark, forcing me to lose sleep while examining every shadowy shape to see if it moved.

For the six years we lived in that house, I didn't tell a soul about my Lady-ghost sitings. It wasn't until we moved all the way across the country to a ghost-free new build that the topic came up, and everyone in my family confessed they'd been seeing

Lady-ghost for years. And, yes, Mom had also seen the man in the basement. How comforting that would have been as a young girl, not to be told that being afraid of the dark is silly and that at bedtime, "lights out, means lights OUT!"

While other kids huddled around a flashlight at sleepovers, squealing in excitement about a ghost story they'd heard, my sightings had removed the veil between superstition and reality. I'd already seen beyond the limitations of both science and religion, giving the supernatural world an automatic seat at my table.

Those hauntings terrified me, but they also cracked open my awareness that there was more to life than a see-it-to-believe-it reality. If anything, my early supernatural experiences produced in me an insatiable curiosity.

In second-grade science class, I raised my hand to ask, "Mrs. Blankenship, how was it possible for God to create the world in seven days if dinosaurs existed millions of years before humans?" I was met with a hesitant, "Umm...well...Micki, you're going to have to ask your parents."

For legal reasons, Mrs. B couldn't tell me that Genesis is a questionable depiction of history, but the leak had been sprung. At eight years old, I felt like I'd made a monumental discovery. *Ah-ha! Wait – why isn't everyone else seeing this?*

My childhood church didn't offer better answers. When I asked my Sunday school teacher about ghosts, I was told in no uncertain terms that the only ghost I needed to worry about was the Holy Ghost. *Sorry, lady...too late for that.* I wasn't trying to be insubordinate, and I wasn't *dabbling* in the "dark arts"; those ghosts came to *me*.

I get it, though. If you've never seen a ghost or if you've grown up believing that what you can see, smell, touch, hear, and taste is all that exists, it's probably hard to imagine how any logical person can accept mystical ideas as reality. But when you've grown up with a ghost as your *roommate*, anything is possible. And while the Bible is full of miracles and unexplainable phenomena, and science spills secrets of the ever-unfolding natural world, they each exclude what I know to be true through felt experience – that the world is and always has been a magical place. And while we can't always derive clear answers and meaning to our experiences, ignoring them is like choosing to live in a grossly limited, two-dimensional quarantine.

After my encounter with the Victorian Lady-ghost, I had multiple run-ins with other formless friends. Portland, Oregon is teeming with them, which I learned over the two years I lived there after college. The restaurant where I worked had a dude-ghost who hung out in my peripheral vision, and at six in the morning, when I was there all alone, he stomp-stomp-stomped up the wooden basement stairs behind me.

On another occasion, I made the mistake of dating a fellow see-er with whom I had a strong, energetic connection, and together, we conjured a rather unpleasant gentleman into our room one night. He wore a striped tailcoat and stared at us from the closet with black, malicious eyes that seemed to be all pupils. This added a new dimension to our already-complex relationship. And while it wasn't the reason we broke up, I didn't add it to the 'pros' column for why we should stay together.

The truth is, life is hard enough when you're dealing with the things you can see. You have to manage yourself and your relationships and figure out how to make a living and keep your body healthy and make sure your cover-up matches your skin tone - all of which feels like a full plate. For see-ers or feelers like me who go through life like a human antenna, constantly picking up signals from the other side, things can get complicated.

After a few unsettling encounters, I decided it was time to simplify my life and made a conscious choice to close the door on my ghostly friends. It was more of a mental reckoning: I welcomed loving guidance and angelic protection, but nothing else. If something brought bad vibes, I was like, *Nope! You need to flip a uey and float away on the goosebumps you rode in on.*

It wasn't until my late twenties that I reignited my curiosity and fully leaned into the woo by enrolling in massage therapy school. There, I opened myself to the spiritual realm in a much bigger way, but this time I treated it like any healthy relationship, with clear boundaries.

The supernatural may have first introduced itself through ghosts I wanted to evict, but I also knew there was more waiting on the other side, the kind of presence I wanted to invite in.

Instead of feeling like a defenseless sea cucumber, constantly reacting to whatever came my way, I discovered new modalities that gave me more control over the energy I allowed in and through me. Through bodywork and energy healing practices, I fine-tuned my antenna. For the first time, I not only learned to tune into frequency with intention, but also how to let it guide me.

In *The Secrets of the Power of Intention*, Dr. Wayne Dyer explains (and I'm paraphrasing) that *every* human has a connection to the divine, but some people have more dirt clogging the channel than others. With meditation, yoga, prayer, and energy work, I learned how to clear that channel, receive the good, and firmly decline the rest.

My guidance now shows up in all kinds of ways. Several years back, a text message popped up announcing a women's retreat in NYC. I'd never done anything like it before, but I knew instantly that I needed to be there. It felt like a deep knowing I had to act on. That one trip became the catalyst for buying my dream home, getting published for the first time, leaving a toxic relationship, traveling the world, and building a successful business.

Sometimes the guidance is as subtle as a simple "tap" to reach out to a friend, and when I do, they'll often say, "Oh my gosh, I was just thinking about you!" With daily practice, the nudges get stronger, and my inner wisdom is easier to hear. And while I don't always remember to pause and tune in before taking action, life is so much sweeter when I do.

Of course, the universe doesn't only nudge me forward in my own unfoldment; sometimes it seats me smack-dab in the front row of the truly bizarre.

When my short-lived massage therapy career ended with a shoulder injury, I was hired by a nutrition company. It was there that my new colleagues introduced me to a whole new kind of sorcery called muscle testing.

With the understanding that our bodies know more than our minds, muscle testing helps determine if a person suffers from underlying food sensitivities, exposure to toxins, deep emotional trauma, or which systems in the body need nutritional support.

This all sounds pretty "out there", but when you see it in action or are the test subject, you discover that what seems like a bullshit party trick is a surprisingly legitimate way to communicate with the body.

It wasn't until I was at a work conference in Wisconsin that I witnessed just how screwed up things get when you treat your body like a Ouija Board.

The Abby Hotel sits on a small lake about an hour outside Milwaukie. I'd traveled there with two other women from the nutrition company for a three-day sales training. I looked forward to spending time with my work friends, Stacia and Anika, who were both adept muscle testers. In the same way teenage girls take quizzes in the back of Cosmo to see who they're going to marry or which sexual position best matches their astrological sign, I planned on tapping into my friends' powers like a crystal ball during our downtime. I'd been feeling a little stuck and was sure they'd test the truth right out of me.

After a long day of sales training, we went to a company dinner. Ron, a bigwig and my boss's new boss, offered to drive us the twenty minutes through Wisconsin farmland. Dinner was fine, but I quickly learned that while my Austin coworkers were all health-conscious muscle testers, the higher-ups ate like garbage and drank like fish, especially Ron, our unlucky ride home.

Swerving on a windy country road under dark skies, I exchanged wide-eyed what-the-fuck looks with my friends. Not only was Ron completely wasted, but with some bro-level flirting and a sob story about his recent divorce, he was clearly angling to sleep with one of us – not that he cared which one.

At long last, we arrived safely back at the hotel. Piling out of the car and into the hotel lobby, my heart was racing, my guts were squirming, and my skin was an ashy green-gray. I looked like E.T. when he was lying in a ditch, too sick to phone home.

Shaking off the night, my friends and I decided to hang out in my room to decompress. I thought, *Oh, goody, it's muscle testing time! I can't wait to see what wonders my body reveals.*

And indeed, it was muscle testing time, but that night, instead of focusing on how to help their dear old friend Michelle, my friends muscle tested to see what the hell was wrong with Ron. You see, they are such good muscle testers, they don't even need the other person or their outstretched arm there to do it! They can do it from a *distance*, using their *own* hands.

It gets much weirder.

Mumble-whispering different questions under her breath, Anika performed the tests. If her outstretched finger became weak beneath the pressure of her other finger, then her statement was false. But, if the finger remained strong, then BINGO! We've got a winner.

Test: Is Ron really going through a divorce?

Finger: Strong = Yes

Me: *Shocker!*

Test: Does Ron have a deadly parasite controlling his brain?

Finger: Weak = No

Me: *Debatable.*

Test: Does Ron have a negative entity attached to him?

Finger: Strong = Yes

Me: *You mean like a spiritual barnacle?*

Test: Is Ron possessed by a pissed-off ghost?

Finger: Weak = No

Me: *Possession would be a better excuse than just being an asshole.*

Test: Does Ron have a demon attached to him?

Finger: Strong = Yes

Me: *Oh, a demon. I'm sure glad that's settled.*

The legitimacy of this test was feeling more questionable by the minute. I mean, I can get on board with testing someone else for a peanut allergy, but testing yourself for someone else's *demon?* Come on!

Together, my God-fearing friends unanimously agreed the obvious next step was to recite a biblical incantation specifically designed to remove the demon from Ron's unsuspecting body. After a quick scroll through her phone, Stacia pulled up a long paragraph she was sure would do the trick.

"If we recite this together, it will be more powerful," she proclaimed.

Anika nodded her head vigorously in agreement, and while I wasn't convinced that Ron had a demon, or if he did, that removing it would make him less of a jerk, I decided to play along. What's the harm in performing a little spell reversal amongst friends?

The low harmonic drone of our voices joined in a rhythmic chant sounded like a coven of witches. I wondered how we would know if it was working or if we'd need to read it more than once. Don't these things have to be done in threes? I was obviously the novice.

As we finished reciting the last word of the last sentence, we heard a loud thump in the bathroom, but none of us felt compelled to get up and investigate. Outside, the wind whipped across the lake, and rain fell with cinematic drama. Titillated from our experiment, we did what any normal trio of women would do on a voodoo business trip; we talked for another two hours about our kids and our husbands and about nothing at all.

Purely exhausted from a long day of training and hob-knobbing and demon thwarting, I was relieved when my friends left to sleep in their own rooms. I just wanted to brush my teeth, wash off my mascara, and fall into bed.

Flipping on the bathroom light, I saw what had caused the thump. Every towel that had been neatly folded and stacked on a shelf nearby was now stuffed into the center of the toilet. I don't mean one happened to fall off the shelf. Defying the laws of physics, the ends of these towels, all three of them, were stuffed deep into the basin. The hair on the back of my neck pricked up and I called down the hallway to Anika, "Get back in here. Y'all put a demon in my room!" I've had friends leave things behind after a visit, like a jacket if they're forgetful or a bottle of wine if they're nice, but a demon? Well, that's just poor manners.

Showing my friends the toilet towels, they didn't skip a beat, as if they dealt with these pesky things all the time. Stacia marched over to the window and pushed it open while she and Anika said a prayer to send the demon out the window and into the stormy night. To be absolutely sure it was gone, they did their due diligence and muscle tested to make sure it was gone.

I was not experiencing the same kind of job-well-done satisfaction they were. Still, with two long days left of the training, I had to get some sleep, so I left my lamp on and covered my eyes with the only towel that had been spared from the commode.

The next morning, the clouds had cleared, and Ron was in an almost sprightly mood. Unaware of the spiritual cleansing we'd performed on his behalf, I studied him closely and noticed he seemed different, lighter, more at ease. Could it be that our little séance changed his life? Would he patch things up with his wife, become a better dad, and start walking the talk of the nutrition business, all because of our kind deed? Can I add that to my expense report for the trip? Imagine the response from HR when they see an invoice for: Airport parking $30, Meals $150, Demon Removal...um, priceless?

I'll never know if we really removed a demon from Ron or if his liver just needed time to drain the vodka martinis from his bloodstream. What I know for sure is that the world we can see is constantly co-mingling with all manner of external forces and beings that influence us in ways we'll never understand.

The idea that everything is made of energy, and all living beings are connected to that energy, isn't a stretch; it's a fact. Believing in angels, spirit guides, and synchronicities just makes sense. (I draw the line at unicorns and fairies because I'm not insane.) You don't have to see ghosts, cast out demons, or meditate on a mountain 24/7 to experience the benefits. When we acknowledge the magic, mystery, and infinite possibilities of the universe while staying in awe of the physical world, we are gifted with a technicolor life, layered with meaning and delight.

For some reason, I am like a divining rod for the weird and woo, and this has clear benefits. With practice, I've learned how to open myself up to attract good people and opportunities. I've discovered immense freedom in believing in the infinite. Assuming that I'm a sparkly little spirit living in a physical body, guided and supported by a great divine frequency (that I interchangeably call God or Source or The Universe), gives me the confidence to take bigger leaps in my life, love wildly, serve wholeheartedly, and have fun doing it.

Over time, I've stopped seeing the spiritual world as something "out there" that could sneak up and shout, "Boo!" and started experiencing it as an invitation to expand. The nudges, whispers, and synchronicities aren't distractions; they're guidance. The divine isn't separate from me; it is the current running through me, reminding me that things are always unfolding in my favor, and that what I focus on grows.

Divine connection guides every step — how I run my business, how I listen when I need direction, how I connect with people, and most importantly, how I trust that I am exactly where I need to be in any moment.

Sometimes I wonder if I had not been shaken by those early hauntings, would I have come to this relationship with the divine at all?

I'm not certain if being a see-er is a trait that's passed down genetically, but my son is also gifted with sight and deep intuition. Fiercely independent and sometimes wise beyond his years, he seems to channel wisdom from ancient warriors and monks. One night, when he was very small, he came into my room to report that a man was peeking at him from his closet and that he had just seen someone move through a wall. I knew exactly what he meant. So, instead of telling him he was only imagining things and that "Lights out means lights out," I filled his pockets with gemstones, burned sage in his bedroom, recited loving incantations, and let him sleep with a light whenever he wanted.

Ultimately, I wanted to give my son what it took me decades to embrace: that the work is never about closing the door on mystery, but about opening to the wonder of knowing we are part of it.

Because when we really open ourselves to the divine, it doesn't feel scary; it feels like love.

MICHELLE SAVAGE

Michelle Savage is an international best-selling author, keynote speaker, and the founder of Sulit Press, a boutique, non-fiction publishing house based in Austin.

Michelle has helped dozens of entrepreneurs, executives and visionaries become bestselling authors in half the time it takes to go it alone - while ensuring exceptional quality and results.

With philanthropy and social impact as a cornerstone of her company, Michelle is proud to donate all proceeds from Sulit's multi-author books to non-profits benefiting children in her community.

She believes everyone has a story worth telling and is passionate about helping them tell it well.

Website: www.sulitpress.com
Instagram: https://www.instagram.com/sulitpressbooks/
Facebook: https://www.facebook.com/SulitPress
LinkedIn: https://www.linkedin.com/in/michelle-savage-43032659/

5

WHEN GOD WRITES THE STORY

BY DEANNA COX

Beyond the stage, it's pitch black, but up here the brightness is unforgiving. Sitting here under the lights, I'm trying to think of an answer that doesn't embarrass me but still tells how I overcame this weakness. I start to sweat, my hands shake, and I feel my voice trembling.

The lights, the silence, the weight of the moment were something I had been building toward for months. Back then, I wasn't on a stage. I was in my pajamas, hunched over my laptop, staring at the same screen day after day. I wondered why I should even get dressed. I wasn't going anywhere or seeing anyone. Even though the sun was shining and the air crisp, I had no one to see and no places to go. Surrounded by paintings of memories gone by, I scrolled through LinkedIn, job sites, and Google. My depression went beyond job searching. The limitations of my age, the burden of my depression, the doubt about my ability, appearance, and personality, the struggles after 2020 swirled in my mind, turning the days into dark nights and dark months. Then, a glimmer of hope. The phone rang.

My first instinct was to let the unknown number go to voicemail, but I answered. "Hello, may I speak with Deanna Cox?" the caller asked. His calm, reassuring tone surprised me. "I'm David Smith from ABC Food Service. We received your resume and would like to talk with you about a position."

I almost hung up, thinking it might be a scam. After months of searching, could this be real? But it was—and soon, I was hired back into the food service industry I loved, consulting with restaurant owners, and moving to a new city to work during the work week. After months of financial stress, illness, and setbacks, this opportunity felt like a new beginning.

With that job came some stability to our lives, but I still had a lot to figure out. My husband was employed, but without my paycheck, money had been tight. Sending all my weekdays away from home was incredibly hard. One evening, while talking with my daughter, she said, "Mom, just move in with us. We have room, and it would be better for you." Though humbling, I agreed, and living with her family reminded me what grace and support looked like in action. Having always been a strong woman, the one who could solve any problem and make it look like it was a tea party, this new life was humbling.

Watching my daughter's faithfulness—getting up every morning at 5:30 A.M. to study her Bible—seeing how supportive and kind her family was to everyone around them, including the three-year-old, inspired me. Still feeling a bit sad and lonely, I sat in the rocking chair in my room and thought about how I used to read the Word, pray, and serve. I no longer did any of these things. Tears, again, always more tears. And then one night, I picked up my Bible again. My daughter was in the living room reading. As I walked in to talk with her, I asked, "Do you have a Bible study I could start?"

"I do!" she said in an enthusiastic voice. She eagerly handed me one that guided me through Scripture. Slowly, I felt God stirring my heart back to Him.

Balancing work in one city while my husband stayed in another was painful, but I began to see God's purpose. He hadn't just led me to a job; He had drawn me closer to my daughter, her family, and most importantly, back to Him. During the week, I stayed with my daughter and her family, but weekends were spent at home. My health and heart felt torn. Being away from my husband, the one I chose to build life with, was hardest of all. We missed the little things: shared dinners, someone waiting at home, the comfort of daily presence. Loneliness settled in for both of us, and we lived for the weekends to feel "normal" again.

While God had already been transforming the major areas of my life, He had one more big surprise in store that I never would have expected.

It was a beautiful day to drive to Austin for a networking lunch. The sun was shining, still warm, and opening the moon roof felt like a summer day from my youth, with loud music blaring and hair blowing in the wind. After lunch, I approached the owner of a boutique publishing company to learn about the process of writing a chapter in her next book. *I'm not sure why I felt I needed to do this, other than it felt like it could help me with my business.* The owner, a sweet, uplifting woman, had become a friend, and I knew she would be honest with me about my story.

That's how I found myself writing a chapter in one of her multi-author books, *Pieces to Purpose*. Writing my chapter prompted me to delve into my past. Memories came flooding back as I wrote about the things I'd stuffed away for decades, like being mentally abused for years by my ex-husband, manipulated, and torn down. He had destroyed my faith and my confidence. I had over twenty years of emotions stuffed away in the trunk of my memories. My chapter became the container to hold them, and I came to trust God's guidance as I told my story on the page.

While I continued to believe in God throughout my marriage, my faith felt distant and unfamiliar. Faith had always been about trusting God—His Word, His power, His forgiveness. I can only assume it was God who eventually helped me leave my abusive first husband and not look back.

As I wrote, my words were scattered, and a clear thought was nowhere to be found. Turning in my first draft was humiliating. My coach called, saying, "Deanna, you are all over the place. Choose what you want to write about, one topic, then throw up on the page with words. We can help you edit from there." I asked for guidance again. "I'll try to write about the experience that will help others. I'll try to share what happened to change my life," I told her. On our second call, she said, "Deanna, try bullet points, it's almost time for the final draft." More consulting, more editing. It was tough love, but I needed it.

Feeling overwhelmed, I sat in my room by the window in the rocking chair. I prayed before I began. Slowly, a light guided my thoughts onto the page. Sending the final copy to my coach, I called her, "I'm done! It needs more work, but I have finished my story!" Pushing the send button on my laptop was freeing! She replied, "I knew you could do it!"

Then, what followed felt like a gift from God.

Writing about experiences from years ago, reliving the hurt, and seeing my children's faces when they read the chapter was torment—but also healing. It helped me see that my past did not define my future. I didn't need to go back; I needed to tell my story to help others see that we can survive the fire and emerge stronger.

It had taken me years to face this part of my life, but when I finally did, I felt a freedom that lifted me like a balloon drifting on the wind. Over time, I discovered a new passion: sharing *Pieces to Purpose* and the struggles of the women in its pages with my community, while also opening up about my own journey to anyone willing to listen. God opened doors in ways I never imagined—panel discussions, podcasts, social media, even the chance to share the book itself. Each opportunity changed me. Each conversation reminded me of why this story mattered. It was a life-altering experience, and I hoped, in some small way, that it touched the lives of those we reached.

During that time, I came to know God again in a real and physical way. Writing sessions with other women in the book became a safe space to share struggles. I said, "I'm so blessed to have found this group, to be able to be honest and raw, releases the hurt that is surfacing from my past." Another author shared, "I feel the same; this is a safe space I feel I can open up, and it helps me move to the next section of my writing." Sharing our stories brought hope and faith. Forgiveness for my ex-husband came more easily than I expected.

One afternoon, sitting outside watching my grandson play, my daughter asked, "Mom, we have a new Bible study starting at Church. Would you like to come with me? It's called Rooted." Hesitant, I replied, "I'd love to go! When does it start?" Walking into that room full of women I didn't know was one of the scariest things I'd done in a long time. "Hello, I'm here for Rooted," I said, trying not to show I was on the verge of tears.

The church was bright and welcoming. The group leader asked me to sit at their table and introduced me to the other women.

She handed me a notebook, saying, "Here is your notebook. We will get into how we use all of the colors of the markers next week." I thought, *Markers? Notebook? Am I at a Bible study or kindergarten?*

The Bible study and book didn't erase my past, but they helped me see I didn't have to live chained to it. These women prayed over me, reminding me that I was loved and seen by God, even in the places I tried to hide. Weekly meetings helped me see that I could tell my story to inspire others. Each week, my heart grew fuller, and I started hearing God again.

Choosing faith meant leaving behind the old version of myself and relationships that no longer supported me. With some family I couldn't walk away from, I slipped back into sadness and darkness—the dark days and nights when my depression was at its worst. For weeks, I struggled, until one day I picked up a devotional that reminded me that faith is stepping into the unknown, holding onto even the faintest whisper from God. I prayed, asking Jesus to draw me back into His light, give me back my peace. And then...I had a revelation.

I realized I had been praying for myself, my plan, not God's plan. Reflecting on Matthew, I remembered: "This then is how you should pray: The Lord is my Shepherd..." He provides, strengthens, guides, and keeps us safe. Calling a friend, I asked, "Why do you think God lets us come and go with our walk with Him?" She said, "So we can grow, become stronger, teach us gratitude, and know He is working on us. We have to trust His timing and His will." I sat in my rocking chair, repeating, "Trust and have Faith, He will lead."

Faith led me out of relationships that no longer drew me closer to God and into places where I had to be honest, vulnerable, and brave. It gave me strength, helped me trust God more deeply, and freed me from fear. One of the authors called, "Deanna, we are holding a women's conference for the authors of *Pieces to Purpose.* Would you like to be on the panel?" That faith carried me onto a stage at a women's conference, where I shared my story from the book. Speaking to strangers was hard, but worth it. Tears and vulnerability connected me with the women God placed in my life. He brought us together to tell our stories so others could find hope in His healing power.

Months after my revelation, I drove to Austin on a beautiful fall day, walking with a light in my heart alongside some of the women who had helped ignite it. At another luncheon, I was asked what I was passionate about. I looked at the owner of the publishing company, "I was passionate about foodservice and serving others through my job. Now, because of YOU, all I want to do is share my story, share the book, and tell how finding my way back to God has changed my life!" She looked stunned. "What did I do?" I was never direct; I looked around the table, and I felt so embarrassed. But it was true—my passion had become spreading the Word of God, which had led me through sharing my story to help others.

When I was asked on stage, "Deanna, tell us about how writing has changed your life and how you became passionate about sharing your story," she said. I smiled, "Writing this chapter in *Pieces to Purpose* meant digging up the broken pieces of my life and healing. Through this process, my passion became helping others to see that they do not need to live in trauma. There is a way out through Jesus and the support of people like us. If my story can help make a difference in one person's life, it was worth the heartache of reliving the hurt it brought back."

During my first panel discussion, I found myself with tears as I answered a question. Afterward, an older lady said, "I loved your story. You touched something inside of me that I have been pushing away for a long time. Thank you for being vulnerable." In that moment, I felt God calling me to continue sharing my story and helping even one person.

A few months later, I'm on another panel with the authors of *Pieces to Purpose*. I am asked while on stage if I have ever lost my voice. With a shaking voice, I say, "I lose my voice and slip away from God more than I would like to admit." Sitting, staring at the lights reflecting on the stage, I continue, "When I feel myself slipping or have let myself slide down the canyon wall completely, I go to someone in my circle. I make a phone call, and I surround myself with the people who help me find peace."

Again, I'm losing my words and tearing up because this is my passion. One of the ladies sitting beside me reaches to touch my hand. I swallow hard, "I am fortunate that I have these women and family who believe I am worthy. I surround myself with people who remind me of my strength. I'm reminded, not by words, but by their presence and their actions, that it's ok to fall, and God is always there to pick us up. It doesn't matter how many times we slide away, He is always there."

Again more women, who have been touched by my words and the story I share, say they feel connected to it. One asks, "How did you sit and dig up your past? It seems it was hurtful." I reply, "It was, and it still is very raw, but if sharing my story helps one person and brings one person to God, it is worth all of the hurt and tears all over again." She hugs me with tears in her eyes.

Sometimes, more often than we know, God sends people to help us through the transition of healing and following Him. When I leave behind certain friendships and family ties, God brings new people into my life—people who encourage me, pray for me, and with me, and remind me of who I am in Him. These relationships aren't just chance; they are exactly what I need, when I need them.

God often replaces what we let go of with something better. He sends the right people to support us at just the right time. During my dark months of trying to find a job, searching endlessly, depression controlling my life, financial struggles, and developing health issues, God sent me to a new city to work— not to be away from my husband, but to be with people who help heal my pain through their stories, showing me there is still hope in the world. He gave me a group of writers who supported me through a tough time. He brought me to a Bible study group that showed me that God lives in us and through us. Now, I recognize when He gives me friends to lean on when I start sliding down the canyon wall. He gives me Grace and the ability to forgive. Most of all, He instills in me a passion to share my story, serve others, and help them see that, through the Grace of God, we are all worthy of a life of happiness and freedom.

Today I am happy and healed. I continue to slide away, but I know how to come back with the Grace of God. I continue to ask for guidance, forgiveness, and to pray, "Not my will, Father, but Yours be done." I use my past to open someone's eyes to what the future can hold for them. I feel the passion to show them, through actions, not just my words, that it is possible to be happy, healthy, loved, and walk with God in life after going through our own Hell.

DEANNA COX

Deanna Cox is a restaurant consultant and owner of Premier Business Consulting, with over 30 years of experience focused on empowering women and uplifting businesses. As a passionate public speaker and best-selling author, she is a member of the Austin chapter of the National Association of Women Business Owners (NAWBO). She is involved in Texas Women in Business, Christian Business Women's Network, and the Texas Restaurant Association. Inspiring others while balancing her commitments to faith and family, Deanna's journey is a testament to creating positive change, driven by purpose, peace, and unwavering faith.

Website: premierbusinessconsultingtx.net
LinkedIn: http://linkedin.com/in/deannacoxtexas
Facebook: https://www.facebook.com/deanna.lemmons/
Instagram: https://www.instagram.com/deannamcox/#

6

FINDING THE ASTRAL PLANE ON THE HIGH PLAINS

BY MICHELLE KRISS

I t was a small hall of justice on the hot, dusty western plains of Kansas, but today it was hosting a first-degree murder trial. I wasn't a juror, but a family member of the deceased, Kristen Marie Trickle. Kristen was a virtual stranger to me. I hadn't seen her in nearly eleven years. I knew of her through other relatives: her gentle spirit, her love of the color purple and all dogs, her controlling husband, and her tragic death. Kristen died in the pre-dawn hours of Halloween 2019. Her cause of death? A gunshot wound under her chin from a .357 hollow point bullet fired from a long-barrel revolver. Kristen and Colby, her husband, were the only two humans in the house at the time she was shot. The State of Kansas alleged that Colby extinguished her beautiful soul in a cold-blooded, greed-driven murder. Colby, and ultimately the coroner, claimed it was suicide. It was a case literally of he said/she said, and she was dead! At the end of this trial, a jury of his peers was to determine which it was.

In the ensuing years between Kristen's death in 2019 and the trial in 2023, my first cousin, Kristen's aunt and maternal figure, had kept me informed of: the grief, the confusion, the chaos, the investigation, the arrest, and the trial date. From the moment the trial date was announced, I *knew* I had to be there. The *why* I could not understand.

On that fall day, armed with a notebook, pen, and a drink, I obediently surrendered my cell phone to a locker and shuffled through the courthouse metal detector. Ahead of me was an older woman with a limp that matched mine, and her shaggy mutt. My left knee screamed at me; it had been hurting for weeks. It was stiff with retained fluid and struggled to bend as I ascended the worn granite staircase to the 3rd floor. Once inside, I scanned the cavernous room and quickly chose a seat on what I thought of as the prosecution's side. As I settled in for the proceedings, I asked myself, again, *Why am I here? Why did I take off work and travel over 200 miles to western Kansas to sit in this courtroom for two weeks?*

The raging conflict between my head and my heart answered alternately. At the time, it was foreign to me, but I now know the voice living rent-free in my head was gaslighting me and attempting to keep me stagnant. She tried for weeks to stop me from even coming. Now that I was here, she was doubling down: *You're here because you're an ambulance chaser! Because it's death and murder and deceit! Because you thrive on pain and drama!* However, the *knowing* deep inside my heart answered calmly: *You are where you need to be. You must make space for this! You have pure intentions.* The answers and the why's would not come for months. On the outside, this was a murder trial. On the inside, this was so much more.

The energy shifted as the attorneys filed in and the bailiff entered. All rise, The State of Kansas v. Colby Alan Trickle, Ellis County Case # 2021-CR-288, the Honorable Judge Glenn

Braun presiding. Immediately, the judge made a light-hearted joke about Catholics. I'm not Catholic or even religious, but it landed like a blow to my knee, and it ached in response. I adjusted my position on the hard pew and massaged my knee in an attempt to move the energy. As I scanned the courtroom, I realized the defense attorney was the elderly lady with the mutt that I followed through security! A dog? Under the defense table? Not a sleek German Shepherd service dog like my wounded-veteran friend has, but a geriatric, shaggy dog of unrecognizable lineage that sneezed, shook, and scratched under the table. There was an irritated buzz in the air as the judge inquired about the dog's bathroom breaks. It seemed like a *lot* of chaos before the opening statements. This was nothing like trials in the movies.

Judge Braun's directions to the jurors resonated through me, and I committed to do what he was instructing them to do: hear all the evidence with an open mind and refrain from forming an opinion until deliberations begin after both parties rest. My body felt alive, awake, and present in that courtroom in a way I'd never experienced before. It was as if *my life* depended on my presence there. As I sat in the courtroom and took in the tales that were being told, something strange started happening. When it began, I didn't quite have the words to explain it, but as I listened to the tales being told, I started to sense Kristen's demure presence sitting beside me. She made her presence known slowly, cautiously, so as not to overwhelm me or make me run in fear.

Day One.

The prosecution's opening statement was simple. The case was ABC: an A)ffair; a B)reakdown of control and C)old hard cash.

Their first witness was the first responding officer at the scene. It was established that there was no body camera footage, only audio on his and the other officers' uniforms that Halloween morning. He further testified that he had been told by dispatch that a man had called 911, saying his wife shot herself in the bed next to him, and that he woke up when the gun discharged. He claimed on the 911 call that there was blood everywhere. The officer was close by and responded to the scene. It was 5:37 am Thursday, October 31, 2019.

The officer's audio was entered into evidence. Then, a pause as the crackly recording reverberated eerily off the granite of the courtroom. The temperature seemed to drop several degrees, and a sudden purple essence swirled through the air, sensed perhaps only by me. A sharp pain stabbed my leg as if an ice pick had been inserted under my kneecap. My ears were listening intently, and my hand was ferociously scribbling the dialogue in the courtroom. Yet, somehow, I wasn't just hearing and imagining it, but experiencing what unfolded as the officer made his way from his patrol car to the tiny house on that cold October morning.

It's 5:39 a.m., and we move swiftly through the darkness, across the dew-kissed grass from the squad car to the tiny house, the officer, Kristen, and me. I'm enveloped in her purple essence as she follows near the responding officer's shoulder, whispering to him through the wind with a potent sense of urgency. The officer's breathing labors in the damp, cold, pre-dawn air, and his uniform swishes as he responds to her prompt by running to the house. On the porch, he speaks to Colby. His voice reverberates cold and lifeless, yet oddly jubilant, as he tells the officer that Kristen and two small, crated dogs are inside the house and that there is blood everywhere.

As the officer enters the house, Kristen urges him to turn to the bedroom where her earthly body lies mortally wounded. Then she and I rush ahead. As he clears the home, his peripheral vision catches the movement of Kristen's foot beyond the threshold of the bedroom door. Gun drawn, he enters the light-filled room, calling out, Kristen! Kristen? Kristen, can you hear me? A small trickle of blood runs down her neck from a small hole under the right side of her chin, but nothing else. Her jaw moves up and down, not to speak merely to summon, like with her foot. He calls out with urgency to his partner, Get the medics in here, NOW! A snapping sound as he dons gloves, checks for a pulse, and then dictates for the audio, ...hands are at side, there's a large caliber revolver perpendicular across her chest.

My knee screamed in pain, my neck stiffened, demanding I leave this place, yet I remained.

Kristen's beautiful purple heart shows me how broken it is, then this message, All I ever did was love him, and this is where we are. I'm controlling this scene, using my power. I'm in charge now!

The pain in my body brought me back to the courtroom, the air thick with tension. I sat on the edge of the hard wooden pew, massaging my throbbing left knee. I listened to the recording, *hoping* they could save her even though I knew it was futile. The sense of urgency was preeminent as the paramedics arrived and quickly decided to move Kristen to the living room for life-saving efforts. Suddenly, a shrill interruption sliced through the voices on the audio, bouncing around the granite-walled courtroom like a pinball. The recording stopped, and questions ensued. The officer testified.

Yes, it was an alarm.

Yes, it was on Kristen's side of the bed.

Yes, it was an iPhone.

Yes, I am familiar with one.

Yes, I stopped the alarm.

Yes, I am sure I did not snooze it.

The district attorney resumed the audio: Rustling could be heard as each of the four moved to grab a corner of the bedsheet, then the officer said, "Wait, let me snap a few pics before we move her." I was suddenly chilled but not sure if it was coming from within or without. It seemed all encompassing, faintly purple. Again, the ice pick twisted under my left kneecap. Under the defendant's table, the dog sneezed repeatedly and scratched incessantly.

Suddenly, I'm again in the tiny bedroom at 505 Mission Mount on Halloween 2019. The scene is fuzzy and confusing. The four of them adjust their positions so the officer can quickly snap a few crime scene photos. The officer points the phone at Kristen's body, and there is a surge of purple energy only I seem to be aware of. The officer's phone is dead. There will be NO photos of Kristen in this bed!

The officer mutters a curse of disappointment, but he's a professional and quickly shifts gears. The tasks are very orchestrated and natural. They're locked-in; it's all about preserving life. I watch as the quartet each grabs a corner of the bedding, swaddling Kristen in it and lovingly move her from the tiny bedroom to the living room for life-saving efforts.

The intensity of the scene and the pain in my body overwhelmed me, and I was no longer able to maintain the connection straddling the past and the present. A bit dazed at losing the 'video', I leaned in, struggling to catch the conversation on the audio bouncing around the courtroom. My hand continued to take concise and faithful notes, almost on autopilot. The voices were muffled by sounds I could not place: ruffling, slurping, and a robotic, rhythmic cadence.

Later that night, I looked through my notes and pondered the journey I had taken. I reread what I wrote of the dialogue between the four officers. My head spun, and certain words jumped off the page at me. Outside, the wind howled, and the sky was purple.

Significant blood and brain matter on my hands

Turn her head

Not consistent with life

Call the coroner

What is that noise? (*In the margin, I'd scribbled, 'another alarm rings.'*)

(*One side of a phone conversation*) *Yeah, back of head blown out...yes, affirmative...we will call it*

Time of death is

Somebody turn off the alarm!

Call dispatch, get the detectives down here

Call the Bureau

As I read these words, I was transported, whisked in a flame of purple, to the living room where Kristen took her final breath.

The female police officer kneels and gently cradles Kristen's head from above, tilting her chin so that an EMT could give rescue breaths. The female officer pulls out her hand and sees blood and brain matter there. One EMT leans over to examine it and says it doesn't look consistent with life.

I suddenly had visuals for the sounds I'd puzzled over earlier in the day:

The ruffling—the male officer's uniformed arms rubbing his body armor near the microphone of his audio.

The slurping—a second EMT suctioning Kristen's airway.

The rhythmic robotic cadence—the male officer's interlocked hands compressing Kristen's rib cage 30 times to every two breaths. Kristen's second alarm, set for 5:45 am, urges incessantly in the background.

The call is made, the coroner concurs, the injuries are not consistent with life. The team stops CPR, and the machines let out a final wheeze before falling mute. There is a moment of complete silence as the quartet of beautiful humans seems to exhale in exhausted unison, gently cradling Kristen as her earthly embodiment is released. A beautiful purple light rises and bathes the room in warmth. It swirled into a tornado, moves to the crates nearby, transmitting love to Roxie and Copper, her beloved dogs...then nothing.

I let out a tense breath, and my body sagged as I returned to the south-facing guest room in my aunt's house. The ink in my notebook was running from the tears that dripped onto the page, and my knee screamed in agony. After limping to the bathroom and wiping my face, I opened the window and collapsed into bed, allowing the Kansas south wind to flow in from the prairie and flush out the heaviness. Again, the nagging question of *Why am I here?* haunted me. My gaslit head replied, *You're here to comfort the family when he gets acquitted.* This record played on, the needle stuck in the loop of the horrific thought. My body responded by restlessly tossing and turning. A soft purple presence shushed me across the wind. *That's not why you're here*, I heard her whisper. *That's not why you're here.* Mercifully, I fell into a deep slumber.

Day Two

A low fog blanketed the landscape, and the air was energetically charged as we drove the ribbon of highway north from LaCross to the courthouse in Hays. We passed a little house on the east side of the road and lamented that Kristen was working towards her dream of turning the shabby, abandoned house and barn into a home-based dog grooming and boarding business. She spoke to my aunt of these dreams mere days before her sudden death 'by suicide'.

The prosecution entered the only crime scene photos of the bedroom, taken after two police officers and two paramedics had moved Kristen's body. In the center was a bare mattress. Kristen's side had a nightstand and her iPhone. The defendant's side: a nightstand with sex toys, Milk Duds, .357 hollow point rounds, a gun safe, and a rifle next to the bed. Although the defendant claimed during the 911 call and on the porch that there was blood everywhere, none was visible. The pillow cradled Kristen's head and absorbed all blood and brain matter. When she was cocooned in the fitted sheet, no remnants of the crime or blood remained in that room.

The coroner's testimony was brief. At the end of his testimony, his reasons for ruling it a suicide seemed to be because: A) it is legally required within seventy-two hours of the death, and B) he had no reason to think otherwise. Her death being ruled a suicide enabled the defendant, Colby Trickle, to collect approximately $130K in life insurance money—$100K from his Army Reserve's spouse SGLI (serviceman's group life insurance) and $30K from her job at Walmart.

Detectives testified that data from the defendant's phone showed he was having a torrid affair online with a female gamer for the twenty-nine months prior to Kristen's death. The testimony was corroborated by a video of the defendant in the police interview room keying into his phone before voluntarily handing it over. His lover had messaged asking if he was available for video sex. His response from the police station after being awakened by a gunshot, after being told his wife was dead, and while her body lay lifeless across town? *I wish I could, but I'm busy right now!* The phone analysis also revealed that on 10/21/2019, just ten days prior, he had googled, *How much is spouse SGLI?* Additional evidence showed that he had only added her to his SGLI policy a mere three months prior to her 'suicide'. In the courtroom, the dog rustled, scratched, and sneezed repeatedly under the defendant's table. Kristen's purple presence was noticeably absent today. They were both as disgusted as the rest of us.

That Halloween, after thirteen hours in the interview room, Colby Trickle's mother picked him up from the police station. Almost two years would go by before he would return to this police station under arrest for Kristen's murder. In those two years, he tried to meet with his online lover, collected Kristen's life insurance money, bought a car, splurged incessantly on online gaming, commissioned a custom $2000, life-size, body-temperature sex doll, and got engaged to a new woman. He had no job, not even the army reserves. We'd learned through testimony that the pittance he received from a one weekend a month and two weeks a year gig had been his only steady income for the entirety of his six-year marriage to Kristen. By August 2020, the defendant's accounts were overdrawn, his car repossessed, and his engagement broken. When arrested in July 2021, he was still living in his mother's basement, gaming all night and sleeping next to his store-bought woman.

Day Three

The courtroom was abuzz after the break. The prosecution's final star witness, a psychiatrist analyzing Kristen's propensity for suicide post-mortem, was vehemently objected to by the defense. The appellate court ruled her testimony admissible in pre-trial proceedings. She testified Kristen was low risk for suicide for many reasons, but among them, the fact that Kristen set two alarms because she had somewhere to be that Halloween morning, and she had spoken of buying a home and starting a business mere days prior to her death. As this witness and the prosecution volleyed questions and answers to lay the foundation, the dog, feeling the energy shift, became restless under the table. Kristen's familiar purple presence enveloped me, my knee aching in confirmation. This time, we didn't go to the house on Mission Mount, but instead, there was a screen of sorts showing me her last night on Earth. She conveyed to me, *This way is easier, less energy.*

I see Kristen playing with her dogs and know she is dreaming of her home-based grooming business. She is opening bags of candy and is excited about seeing all those precious costumes. She chats with Colby about his mother's Halloween party and sets 2 alarms for work in the morning before retiring to bed. She is so happy to be back in Hays, and for the first time in a long time, she feels hope!

After the proceedings ended, we were all gathered in the first-floor conference room: my sequestered relatives, their supporting family and friends, the prosecution, the lead detective, Kristen's purple presence, and me. The prosecution brought up the option of offering a plea in the morning, when they rested their case. Kristen was patient and gentle, trying to comfort each of them as they wrestled with the idea. Normally, I am one to try to help, but I resolved to remain mum on this matter. I didn't have a dog in this fight. As the discussion continued, my mind drifted curiously to when I heard Elizabeth Smart speak in Florida. Abruptly, as if I'd been overtaken, embodied, my mouth opened and I relayed to the family something similar to what Elizabeth's mother had told her after she returned from her traumatic kidnapping, "The best revenge is having a good life. Don't give him any more of your energy."

Kristen also transmitted this enigma to me in that conference room, but it would be months before I deciphered it.

From the moment Colby pulled the trigger, my eyes were opened. I suddenly saw all the red flags I had been warned about. I had given my whole heart to him and our marriage. Being back in Hays with family made my heart swell with love for all of you and hope for the future. My final hours were spent with my beloved dogs, planning for Halloween, and dreaming of decorating for Christmas. When he shot me, I resolved to comfort and protect all of you, and to make sure he paid for his crime. That is why I moved, not because I was suffering but to protect you from the agony of seeing a photo of me in that bed, so that those four officers, not Colby, would be with me when I transitioned. Colby's chaotic behavior— the spending, and the difficult investigation— I was in charge. The icing on the cake, Colby's court-appointed defense attorney has a dog! You see, dogs can sense things humans can't, and, most importantly, Colby isn't a 'dog person', so I made sure he drew the attorney with the dog!

Day Four

The expert witness was on the stand again today for cross-examination by the defense. After the lunch recess, the prosecution rested: no plea had been or would be offered. The defense made a motion for acquittal, claiming the state had not proven its case. The motion was denied, and the defense began putting on its case. Kristen sat next to me, demurely, as her soft voice and gentle demeanor resonated through the courtroom as she spoke to a debt collector. In the margins of my notes, I wrote, *This testimony seems to be supporting the prosecution!* A light brush across my neck and a sharp pain in my left knee confirmed my conclusion. Kristen was fully in control of the proceedings.

Day Five

It was Friday, mid-afternoon of the first week of the trial that was scheduled for two weeks. The defense confirmed Colby would not be testifying on his own behalf and then rested their case. The dog shuffled under the defense table as the judge instructed the jury before sending them to deliberations. No one was sure what to expect this late on a Friday afternoon. *Would it spill over until Monday?* Just over two hours later, the jury returned, having unanimously agreed. Colby murdered Kristen in cold blood.

As I reviewed, retold, and recounted the story during the winter of 2023, I became more and more aware of Kristen confirming pieces of the puzzle I'd accurately filled in. I gradually started to understand *why* it was so important for me to be at the trial. I was to deliver a message. My next question was, *who?* Who was the message for? Sometime late fall, around Halloween, I felt I had a good grasp on the message so I decided to try it out on her grandmother. I nervously texted my aunt and asked to speak to her. She asked why, suspiciously. My resolve was waning. *Could I do this? Could I say all of this to my aunt? Would she call me crazy? Would I call me crazy? Did I believe all of this?* Suddenly, that seemed important. *Did I believe in this experience? Was it real? Had I really gotten to know Kristen? Had she really sent me a message?*

A version of me said *it's a fairy tale,* but a purple flame inside of me confirmed it was a deep knowing. It was the reason women were burned at the stake. It was the reason women were murdered in cold blood for cold, hard cash. A woman with a beautiful heart like Kristen, connected to other women with beautiful hearts - like her family she'd missed so much - could move mountains. They could claim sovereignty and build Queendoms with or without kings. At this point, I was relieved when my aunt asked me to text the message, as I'm sure my voice would have betrayed me.

I typed out a long message, my body trembling, my throat constricting, and my neck tensing as I hovered over the send button. All of those sensations in my body distracted me from the feeling that a hot metal blade had been inserted under my kneecap. This was the precipice of my fears, and something was definitely trying to hold me back from opening this vault! I hit send and waited nervously for a reply, chaotic energy buzzing all up and down my spine. A lump formed in my throat, my chest tightened, my belly rumbled. I had the urge to pee, to poop, and-oddly- was suddenly horny? The three dots popped up. I held my breath. *Ding.* Short and to the point, "I already knew this. Kristen's told me." She was not *who* the message was for.

That left the more difficult of the two choices, my cousin. She was the closest thing to a divine mother Kristen ever had. The one Kristen loved unconditionally and vice versa. The challenge was connecting to her; Kristen couldn't get the message through. Suddenly, I had an answer to a question I'd not previously considered: *why me?!* She needed someone in the physical world. She had chosen me, the open-minded black sheep cousin, to come in and bridge the gap between the divine and the physical. Kristen needed me to tune into her frequency, to receive and decode an enigma, and to transmit a message.

What a challenge this would be as my cousin is devoutly religious, works in a church her husband pastors, and is not into hippy dippy alternative dimensions. Truth be told, I wasn't really much into them at that point in my life either. I was open to the idea, but never really pursued it for myself. Suddenly, I was telling stories of purple flames and becoming intimately connected with someone who is no longer physically embodied.

I began slowly, outlining that we could use a stoplight, red, yellow, and green. The first issue was her believing I even had a message from Kristen. We've had numerous conversations since the trial, but in writing this, I have realized this *is* the message. I have finally delivered it fully.

About six months after the trial, another answer came to the question of *why me?* I have learned to trust the messages of my *own flesh-and-bones house*, taken tally of all the scores that have been kept there, and gained the confidence and know-how to burn down those versions that no longer serve me. I now fully embrace the hippy dippy divine power that has awakened inside of me. It is a mature, divine feminine power that transcends space and time, that has allowed me to embrace and alchemize my darkness. My knee seldom throbs to confirm my connection.

My body has gentler ways of summoning me now. Kristen has moved on, but she can be reached; I know her frequency.

Prologue: Colby Trickle is serving life in prison and will not be eligible for parole until 2073. Kristen's little house on the east side of the highway, south of Hays, remains abandoned.

MICHELLE KRISS

Michelle is a writer, ritualist, and reclamation artist devoted to truth, embodiment, and the sacred unraveling of old paradigms. Her work explores the tender terrain between trauma and transcendence, drawing from her lived experience as a mother, survivor, builder, and mystic. Michelle channels wisdom through both structure and chaos—renovating homes, relationships, and inherited myths with equal courage and craft. Her storytelling interweaves ancestral threads, erotic sovereignty, and feminine intuition, inviting readers into deeper intimacy with themselves and the world. She is the creator of mythic frameworks, couples retreats, and sovereign rites of passage that ignite personal and collective transformation. Whether through writing, ceremony, or design, Michelle stands at the precipice of the personal and the planetary—helping others cross with reverence, rage, and radiant aliveness.

7

WHEN THE DIVINE SPEAKS

BY SHAY MICHELLE DRAPEAU

The Bible is a powerful work written by flawed men, but as a young girl, I thought it held the only answers. It was the definitive book on right and wrong, the difference between saint and sinner. Based on what I'd seen in movies or heard from family members, church was a place to lay your burdens down, heal your body, and fill yourself with the holy spirit. It looked like your best clothes, community, support, and good food. Worship was singing, praise dancing (choreographed or in the aisle), and reciting scripture.

As a young girl, I *begged* to go to church. Not because of what I knew of the Bible. I wanted to feel the Holy Spirit take over my body and fill me with the Lord, just like in the movies. Every Sunday, we went to All Saints Southern Missionary Baptist Church. I attended with my grandmother, aunts, and cousins. It was a beautiful presentation of worship. Communion every first Sunday. The Motherboard, a group of women elders who had prime seating in the front row, ran the church and the children. A deacon's wife, Mother Davis, sold candy. She was my favorite. We dressed in our Sunday best, but went above and beyond for

Easter Sunday. My granny would cook after service, except on Communion Sunday, which was the day the Motherboard cooked for the congregation.

I wanted nothing more than to be baptised. I didn't know what it was, but I knew it was a special day. You were dressed in pretty white robes, blessed by the pastor, and dunked in water. At twelve, the significance of the act was completely lost on me. I wanted to feel special. I wanted to be in the Lord's house as his child. I had yet to have sins in need of washing away, but I wanted to be the center of the Holy attention. I shared the day with parishioners of other congregations, as our church didn't have a baptism pool. It wasn't long after that day that I began sleeping in on Sundays, having leveled up, in my mind. I'd taken the magic Super Mario mushroom that brought you closer to God. Why keep learning the word when I was bathed in Holy water? I got what I came to church for: attention and salvation. A baptism without a full understanding of your religious self leaves you wanting and unfulfilled. Hindsight has taught me that a shortcut to salvation didn't exist.

I tried to be a good religious girl again in college. I found a group of devout women and joined them in the campus choir. But going to church, even just to perform, felt like lying. I could find myself in every sermon, yet I constantly compared my faith and beliefs to the women next to me in the pew. My faith wasn't strong enough because I questioned everything. Seeing the way others worshipped, knowing that there are more than Baptists and Catholics in the world, piqued my spiritual interest. Away from home, I got to make my own decisions about my faith, so I added a class on ancient religions to my schedule. While I fell asleep in class most mornings, it prompted a new perspective on global religion. Gods and goddesses I wanted to learn more about. Rituals and rites of passage that were foreign to my Baptist upbringing.

The quest raised more questions than answers. *If God isn't the only Higher Power, which do I worship? How do I know God's plan for me? Do other gods have plans as well? Why would God allow that to happen to his son?*

My aunt Clarice, who'd been like a surrogate mother in New York, was always willing to help answer my questions. A Christian woman, she saw who I was but never made me feel like I had to believe what she did. She answered my questions so that I could make up my own mind. I accepted that questioning one's faith is an act of faith in itself– to trust in something you don't fully understand.

After I was married, I gave up the church and my search for awakening yet again. Since my partner's faith was broken by his experiences with multiple houses of worship, I didn't dare seek my own understanding. I felt the need to "stand by my man," recalling the teachings of my old church, that a man and woman could not reside as man and wife if they did not hold the same beliefs. I found myself battling between my desires to hold on to my beliefs, be a good wife by aligning with my husband's lack of religious practice, and uphold societal expectations.

When my friend K, who was also the mother to my godsons, came for a visit, she was super stressed about her sons. While we went out on the town, my family stayed with her two boys. Unable to handle the repeated meltdowns of her youngest, my family called to bring us home. Frustrated, K had her own meltdown on the ride home. She'd been having trouble with both boys' behavior for months and was at her wits' end. When we arrived, we were informed that her youngest child had been having meltdowns over the smallest things. I watched as my child accidentally spilled water. My youngest godson tracked into the puddle, soaking one of his socks. He dissolved into a frenzy of wails and kicks. My then-husband approached him, trying to calm him down. Noticing that he was kicking as if to flick something off, my ex reached down and pulled the wet sock from his foot. The wails and kicking ceased.

I calmly said, "He's on the spectrum, K. He's small and sensitive, and you have to be his advocate. He needs you to take your head out of the sand because you're the only one who can fight for him." I didn't know where those words were coming from, but after the first few came out, I couldn't stop. It was a verbal convulsion. "You're the only one who knows that sweet little Black child isn't difficult. He isn't a problem. He doesn't have behavior issues. He's a kid in a world that doesn't make sense to him. He's a kid in a world where he doesn't know how to communicate, evaluate, or navigate. You have to do that *for* him. You have to start now, while he's young enough to start out on the right path."

I stood in my kitchen, not knowing where the words were coming from, but my friend stood there and listened with tears tracing her cheeks.

A chill ran down my spine as I felt a weight leave my body.

"Shay..."

"No." I stopped her. "That wasn't me. I don't know where that came from. But it wasn't me. *Someone* needed you to hear that."

It was the first time I'd ever leaned into letting words that didn't belong to me leave my lips without analyzing or editing. I often spoke my mind. When I did, it was based on my lived experience. I had none in this instance. I didn't have a child on the spectrum. I didn't have a child with sensory issues. I didn't have a child who only communicated with their parents. Even now, recalling her tear-stained face, I know I did the right thing. The message wasn't mine to hold.

Fearful of what it meant, but curious about its power, I explored what it meant to receive such downloads. When I learned that our ancestors speak to us, I immediately thought of the movie Mulan. Her ancestors sent her a guide. How could I find my own?

When I received the message for my friend, my body didn't seize; it was still, calm. I became a vessel, a messenger. Now, when it happens, it's like an itch in my brain that can only be scratched by going through a maze of verbal releases. Each word brings relief as I move closer to the goal.

About seven years ago, I met a woman at a hobbyist conference. Our sisterhood was light, marked with fun, fleeting chats, and the occasional Facebook comment. Years later, we crossed paths in a mindfulness workshop, quietly recognizing each other in the Zoom chat after she spoke of her son and empty nest, a brief but familiar exchange.

That night, as I meditated, I held a vision of her. She was standing in front of a shop with Japanese characters. How I knew they were Japanese, I still have no clue. A man held her hand. He leaned in, pulling her closer. He kissed her. I couldn't hear their words, but their body language screamed intimacy. Colors flowed around them, glowing reds and purples.

I messaged her through Facebook. It felt like an intrusion, but something told me she needed to know what I saw. I told her she didn't have to believe me, that I don't fully understand it myself. I laid it all out for her. She replied that she was going to Japan with her son and his wife in just a few weeks. She hoped the someone from my vision would be her forever partner.

As a believer, she received the message well. We talked about receiving downloads.

Her: *Have you ever tried connecting with your ancestors?*

Me: *No. How do I do that?*

Her: *There are a lot of ways. You could meditate, read cards, etc.*

Me: *Cards? Like tarot?*

Her: *Oracle cards. Abiola Abrahms has an Oracle deck. You should check it out.*

The ancestors speak.

The deck was called the African Goddess Rising deck. The accompanying book spoke of ancestral connection in the form of African and Caribbean lineage–connecting to Goddesses and icons. I found the guidance to be in alignment with the woman I wanted to be, the advice the former elders gave, and the fire in my spirit. It opened my creativity and allowed me to shift my perspective on what it means to listen from another plane.

One of my first readings was the Goddess Temple Spread:

"What does my soul need me to know?"

Iset, Goddess of Surrender - I chose to surrender to my grief. I let it bubble over no matter when it hit me. I went back to journaling *to* my emotions, opening myself to every facet, angle, and position my emotions held.

"What am I really thinking or feeling?"

The Seven Sisters, Goddesses of Creativity - I need to get back to writing. Creating is healing to my soul. I wrote, I sang, I danced, and I played.

"What is happening with me physically?"

iNkosazana, Goddess of Celestial Alignment - I chose meditation to balance my body. I went to a Reiki healer to learn where I was blocked. My throat and my heart. In celestial alignment, I found it easier to cut ethereal cords and create boundaries.

Divine alignment came to me through those readings. I accepted the memory that I'd been down this path before. I found solace when I received the "go-ahead" I was looking for to accept myself as an empath.

I was on vacation in Hawaii with my family. It was our second visit to be riddled with illness. There was only one day when none of us were sick. Wanting to see more than the hotel next door, I suggested we venture out to explore the island. We decided our historical portion would be Pearl Harbor. The museum was vast. Much of it outdoors, we followed the tour guide to a platform. On a wall, there were the names of soldiers. I knew I'd had soldiers on my father's side and wondered if I'd find their names listed. Seeking connection, I searched that wall until I found a name I recognized. I took the opportunity to test my abilities. Not knowing what I was doing, desiring a connection to an ancestor, I allowed myself to see and hear what history was steeped into those waters.

While my family took in more of the area, I quieted my mind as I allowed my gaze to soften over the water. I opened my hands in front of me. "I am here," I said to the water. "I am healed. I am here to hold." I invited their pain, and I let go of myself, reaching out with my mind and heart. I felt a rush of cool air on the hot day. Fire and mist swirled in my vision as cries rose over the water. I was overwhelmed with anger, fear, and pain. There was thick sadness for the lives that could have been. The sons who didn't get to grow into fathers, fathers that wouldn't be there to guide their children, and brothers who would be mourned by their comrades. They were lost that day. Men who thought they would return home.

I'd never felt a power so great pass through me. I closed my eyes, breaking the bond. I rubbed my tingling hand on my clothes. I found myself deflated. Defeated. *How could I wield a power so great? This kind of ability is meant for someone else.* I had learned to keep myself small. This power required an audacious spirit willing to feel more of that. My heart broke and wept for those lost there, and I didn't know what to do with my anger, sadness, and fear. I had no guide. I was fearful of returning to the Bible for answers, despondent that the words would confirm me as sinful for making such connections. I closed myself off. Not just to landmarks of great devastation, but to all my empathic abilities. I lived in spiritual discontent until the Universe forced my hand and my spirit to reopen and reconnect.

Over the following two years, my family suffered loss after loss. The deaths of family and friends filled my calendar with burials, memorials, and condoling phone calls. At some point, it became too much, and I stopped allowing myself to grieve. By bottling it up and closing myself off, I left no room for the Spirit to comfort me or conjure visions...or so I thought.

It was on a beautifully warm and calm morning in August when I got the call that changed everything. As I did most mornings, I welcomed members into the co-working space where I worked, refilled the sundries and snacks, and chatted with the owner. When it was finally my time to get down to my entrepreneurial work, I received a call from my mother.

"She's gone!" she wailed into the phone.

"Mom!" I yelled over her sobs, unnoticed by those working. Not even a concerned, raised eyebrow. "What happened? Who's gone?"

I walked into the vestibule for privacy.

"My sister. He killed Michelle."

My phone and my knees met the grainy doormat. I couldn't comprehend it. Gone. Killed. As in murdered? No. My family couldn't take this. This is too much on top of so much loss. My mother had just lost a cousin, a best friend, and a colleague. How could this be the next blow?

The loss that finally brought me back to my knees, and my mother's home, was my aunt Michelle.

Michelle died one week after her sixtieth birthday. She and my mother were to have a joint birthday party. Thirty years (less one day) my senior, my aunt was a young spirit. She loved to dance and socialize. Her sons were everything to her. She loved her nieces and nephews as her own, calling to check up or staying on the phone while you commuted home from your late shift. My Teetee.

At home, I sobbed for two days. I went to my hometown alone. I gathered with my mother, her sisters, and my cousins at the funeral home. We were to view Michelle's body before cremation. I hadn't seen a dead body since my brother's funeral more than seventeen years prior.

My mother's gentle words, spoken over her sister, brought me back to the present. My aunts and cousins were taking pictures of and with her, taking clippings of her hair. Taking photos of or with the deceased was a practice I'd only ever seen at my best friend's funeral in New York. It was foreign to see my elders embrace such an act. My body stayed, but I wanted to leave.

"Guess what my name is online," I asked my Teetee over FaceTime a few months before.

"I know you call yourself Shay now. I like it. It's cute."

"Well, I decided to go a bit further and honor one of my aunts. You."

Her smile spread as I claimed the name Shay Michelle.

As I sat in the room with her body, I searched for her presence. Ignoring the ones I came there to comfort, I allowed my grief to wash over me. Off to one side of the room, it was cooler. There she was, watching her sisters lay kisses on her forehead. My Teetee sat, legs crossed at the ankle, her hands pressed anxiously between her thighs, a look of sad confusion as she studied the scene. There wasn't a glow, just yellow. She wore yellow—the color of curiosity and the free spirit.

After losing too many relatives in a short period without room to grieve, I sought solace in connection with my elders and pre-descendants through readings. I went back to the cards. I created an altar. My elders' ashes and photos sit with candles. I invite them in. Yet still, a niggling voice remains that it's against God to play at such things. Would my Higher Power not want me to embrace the gifts he's given me?

I refuse to believe that God would bestow me with a sinful connection to this Universe. This gift given to me is one to be learned, practiced, and embraced. I know that what I feel is the true magnitude of Spirit. When I can't go on anymore, I'll receive a check-in call from my best friend. When I think that the world is too big and too loud, I'm offered the opportunity to rest with my fellow authors. When I know it's time to shed the negativity in my life, people will show me who they truly are, so I can freely let them go.

The Divine gives me a purpose by using me as a vessel. Though it is my earthly thoughts that interpret what is present, I know the choice of delivery is my own doing. I open myself to it. I connect to women who are on the same frequency. I found music and karaoke. I danced with divorceés. I cooked. I cleaned. I cried. I kissed. I published!

Downloads are just as much for the person in the vision as they are for the empath herself. I have learned that the purple smoke in my vision signifies a new or blossoming love. It also hints at a strong connection to a Higher Power. Red is for the Root Chakra, for grounding and stability. I am always in transition, learning to love myself and my gifts again. I've accepted my Divine power and I embrace it. I crave a full understanding of what I was getting myself into, what doors I am opening.

The heart chakra serves as a sacred bridge between the body and the spirit. Mine had been fractured for so long that I was no longer in harmony with the Divine rhythm my body and mind required. But I have returned to stillness. I meditate with sacred intention. When my emotions are too heavy, or I carry the weight of others, I surrender them to the page. I relieve my soul in ink. The energetic imprints that sat on my throat and heart silenced my voice and veiled my connection. Now, with a balance of head, heart, and body, I have learned to live in Divine alignment and share my voice.

A shift emerged when my affirmations became a daily twenty-minute meditation, focused on self-love. I embrace loving my body, my powers, and my ability to connect with others. Still, questions of who or what was controlling things remained.

As my marriage came to an end, I began my search anew. How could I find this connection to God whom I'd yearned for in my youth if I were aligned with practices I believed the church would condemn?

The connection with the Divine feels like a warm and cozy home. After years of being small, I spent years beating myself up for not standing out. Now, I lean into the words that download. Many messages I've thought were meant for others have guided me as well. I don't let the faith of others hold me back from my practice. Their relationship with a higher power is not mine. They receive their messages in their own way.

I've taken the time to learn from my fellow empaths. I protect myself from intrusive downloads with frankincense. I sit up and listen when my ears ring. I recognize that my interpretations are based on my lived experience. I'm not a witch or Wiccan. I'm not sinful to listen to what is given to me. There is guidance in the Bible, the Quran, and other religious texts. Connecting to my ancestors is a religious act.

I know exactly where I belong. I know what moments are meant for me. I know the path I should be on. I show up as the Divine by delivering what finds me. I don't always know what they mean, or what the receiver will do with it, but I am in service of conveying the message.

I accept my calling. No more playing small. No more ignoring my gifts. I stand in my power. I embrace the Divine.

SHAY MICHELLE DRAPEAU

Shay Michelle Drapeau is a bestselling author, certified personal development coach, and founder of She Breathes Life™, a movement and community dedicated to helping women and femmes reclaim their voice, worth, and wellness. Known for her warm, bold approach, Shay creates safe, soul-nourishing spaces for healing, storytelling, and midlife resets—guiding those navigating transition, trauma, or transformation with empathy and power.

She is one of the bestselling authors of *Got A Light,* a multi-author book sharing stories of moments that sparked personal change. Through her coaching programs, podcast, and live workshops, Shay supports women in rewriting the narratives they've outgrown and breathing life into the next chapter.

Whether she's holding space for truth-telling, teaching women to set boundaries like a queen, or helping creatives rediscover their spark, Shay shows up with heart, humor, and hope—reminding us all that healing is possible, purpose is personal, and you are always worth the rewrite.

Website: www.shebreatheslife.com
Instagram: www.instagram.com/shebreatheslife
Linkedin: www.linkedin.com/in/sharondrapeau

8

DESPERATELY SEEKING SELF

BY CARRIE QUINTANILLA

I t's 6:00 a.m. on a Saturday, but sleep is the last thing on my mind. I'm in a cavernous hotel ballroom in Cancun, barely lit, the edges swimming in darkness. The air has the bite of a walk-in freezer, seeping through my blanket and raising goosebumps along my arms. I'm wide awake on five hours of sleep and no coffee. The space hums with the low, electric vibration of 2,100 people breathing, shifting, settling into their chairs. Muffled sounds feed the tension - a cough, quickly stifled; a flicker of nervous laughter. Deep inhalations and audible sighs are swallowed by the charged stillness, the kind that hangs in the air just before a thunderstorm breaks.

The lights dim further. A woman begins to sing, her beautiful yet haunting voice saturating the air, seeping under my skin. From the stage, a commanding, very familiar voice cuts through the room, "Sit up, eyes closed. Take a deep breath and R-E-L-A-A-A-X." And so, a multi-hour meditation begins that seems to last only minutes. In the darkness, there is no past, no future - no time at all, really. I'm just here, now. Immersed in the sound, the endless nothing, and the collective presence that fills the room. Am I doing this right? All around me, I hear soft crying, deep breaths, loud sighs of relief – like years of pain being exhaled all at once. I'm trying to trust the process. Why can't I drop in like others seem to so easily?

Then I hear it: "Come back to me." And I realize that I am coming back, because I did indeed go somewhere else. Not to sleep, just not here. His voice continues, "Come back to the room, and when you're ready, you can open your eyes." As I open my eyes and refamiliarize myself with my surroundings, I laugh a little, thinking, *who is this person? And how the hell did I get here?*

The truth is, I've been inching toward this moment for decades, picking up pieces of insight and trying to put the puzzle together. Each trauma, experience, and new challenge chipped away at who I wasn't, so I could finally start to see who I am.

The first memory I have of this was when I was just fifteen. I was a sophomore in high school, deep into figuring out who I was and what I believed about the world, when I attended an Erhard Seminars Training (EST) weekend with several women in my family. EST focused on taking radical responsibility for your life. Your story is not who you are. You are not your past, your circumstances, or your excuses. Even as a teenager, I felt both the weight and the freedom in that idea.

The days were long, the sleep was short, and everything about that weekend felt intense in a way I couldn't fully name at the time. We were staying in a big hotel in Austin, and every morning we'd shuffle down to the ballroom before the sun came up, still bleary from the night before.

One morning stands out vividly. Most of us looked like we'd rolled straight out of bed — sweatpants, messy hair, no makeup, eyes still adjusting to the lights. But one young woman, a few years older than me, showed up polished: full face of makeup, perfectly styled hair, wearing "an outfit." It was obvious she'd been up for a while getting ready. The facilitator called her to the front of the room and asked, not unkindly but directly, "How long did it take you to get ready this morning?" She answered quietly, "About an hour." Then he asked, "Why do you need to be completely made up to come here today? Is this a mask you wear when you show yourself to the world?". She was stunned into silence, and I remember shrinking in my chair. At fifteen, I was already tangled up in questions about beauty, self-worth, and my own values and boundaries. Was it better to show up polished and perfect, and possibly fake? Or to show up as your flawed self – vulnerable, honest, and undeniable imperfect? I wasn't sure yet, but I didn't want to feel fake. That weekend planted a seed. It taught me that only I choose how I show up, and I am not the victim of my circumstances.

This came at a critical time, as some very heavy shit was unfolding in my young life. It started with divorce and quickly unraveled into deeper wounds. My parents had split up when I was seven, and what followed felt like emotional abandonment. My dad moved in with his girlfriend – someone who clearly didn't know what to do with my sister and me. I never wanted to be alone with her. Her behavior was erratic, and she told me bizarre, outlandish lies - including that she had been meant to be my mother. I had never loathed an adult before, and the toll it took on me was real. I dreaded our visits and eventually asked my mom if we really had to go back. Just when I was learning to cope with this woman, she was diagnosed with cancer. She deteriorated so quickly, as if the disease was devouring her from the inside out. When she finally passed, I felt relief, followed by crushing guilt.

At home, my stepfather enforced a strict set of rules that were absurd and offensive to me. I did more than my share to help around the house, care for my sister, and help hold things together. I was not a problem that needed to be managed. I was exhausted, stressed, and fed up. And no one was coming to save me. I kept stuffing the anger, helplessness, and guilt down deep until it crushed me.

The "me" that I tried to be just disappeared beneath the noise. I had to push against everything, try on different identities, and make some dicey decisions just to feel out the edges of who I might be. My appearance, my priorities, and my whole demeanor changed. The "good girl" mask I had carefully crafted through years of pleasing, achieving, and holding it all together, transformed as I forged something new. Harder. Wilder. Less safe. A new persona steeped in self-destruction. Preppy gave way to goth, with my love of black clothes and cobalt blue Henna over box-dyed black hair. In case you were wondering, that combination doesn't fade – it has to grow out! I no longer took pride in my grades, often skipping school to go to Barton Springs on warm days. I plotted how many days I could skip as a senior and still pass all my classes. I was never going to go to college, so it wouldn't be a problem.

My boyfriend suffered from his own baggage and only reinforced my angst and despair. My stepdad was out of the picture by now, but my challenges with my mom were escalating. She was settling into a rhythm, trying to reclaim some version of "normal" in the midst of chaos. But I didn't know what normal was anymore. Everything felt artificial, like we were all pretending darkness hadn't touched us. I had been ejected from childhood too early, forced to carry adult emotions and responsibilities before I had the tools to handle them. For two years, my life had been full of turmoil, trauma, and hypocrisy. Do as we say, not as we do. Keep up appearances. But playing along made my stomach turn. I couldn't squeeze myself into that box. I was pushing back loudly in every area of my life. My mother wanted stability. I wanted authenticity, even if it was ugly. She saw rebellion; I felt like I was fighting for myself.

There was a final conversation. Pent up anger and frustration came gushing out in a torrent of words we couldn't stop or take back. I don't remember the details, but it focused on the boyfriend and "my life choices," and it ended with the "not under my roof" ultimatum. And that was it. I moved out of the house, completely on my own at seventeen. I was untethered and edging toward something dangerous that seemed to have a gravitational pull I couldn't resist. I numbed every emotion and relished in distraction so I wouldn't have time alone to think. I found my share of trouble and "friends" who encouraged it, as well as boyfriends I had no business dating. Some were passive and stayed at arm's length, while others bought front-row seats to my self-destruction - throwing gasoline on the fire just to see how high the flames would go. And I stayed. Much too long. All in the pursuit of finding a version of myself I could believe in.

Coming through that dark time was a defining moment in my life. As I dealt with trauma and heavy adult emotions of my late teens, I had utterly abandoned myself. I had been vulnerable and lost, but not able to ask for help. I had tolerated too many destructive people and situations, as my inner compass was screaming at me to leave. One day, something inside me just broke. I woke up on New Year's Day in a hotel room that I'd paid for, to the putrid smell of a margarita machine I had rented but not yet cleaned, mingled with food I had also purchased and set up. I was hungover, and the sun shone much too brightly through the dingy, grey curtains. The room was a war zone of indulgence: glasses and bottles everywhere, sticky countertops, and a smear of something that looked like queso on a chair. Several of my friends were still passed out on the other bed and the stiff polyester couch. I took in full stock of the room and knew two things. First, I may never drink another margarita based on how the kitchen smelled. Second, these people were not friends. They showed up because I took care of everything, because I made it easy for them to be in my life. Many of them took full advantage - carelessly slighting me, making jokes at my expense, never showing up when I needed them. I kept waiting for someone to notice I was drowning, to care enough to reach in and pull me out. But the truth was, the trouble I was in suited them just fine. It was the toxic glue holding our tangled web of relationships together. When that truth took hold, so did the anger. What the hell was I doing? How long was I willing to live like this? No one was coming to save me. If I wanted out, I would have to be the one to pull myself free.

The anger felt good and righteous. I felt an immediate shift inside. New boundaries snapped into place with a vengeance. I knew who I was. I knew who I wasn't. The veil lifted. Everything sharpened into focus. It felt like a soul recalibration. Like something ancient inside me had finally shaken off the dust and said, "Enough." I severed ties with toxic patterns and people in a single, ruthless sweep. Many of my "friends" were dumbfounded as I stopped showing up, stopped returning phone calls – just stopped. I started a new job in a bigger company and made new friends. In less than a year, my entire circle of friends changed, and the co-conspirators from my darker days were gone. I formed new relationships with people I enjoyed, respected, and even admired. As I made these changes, I became more and more certain that I was on the right path. I had finally learned what that felt like.

As I shook off the numbness, I learned to deeply trust that inner knowing that had guided me for years. Call it intuition or something more mystical. Like an internal compass, it influenced daily decisions on what to put my energy into. This helped me excel at work and was instrumental in helping me take on new roles and responsibilities. When it aligned with something I was passionate about, results weren't just successful – they were extraordinary. Ideas clicked, energy surged, and outcomes consistently outshone even the most ambitious goals. As much as it steered me toward things I was aligned with, it pulled me away from things that were not for me. When it conflicted with something happening in my life, I became restless, depleted, and constantly searched for the next right step. Up to this point, I had appreciated my intuition as a helpful guide, but I had not yet recognized it as the sacred force it was becoming.

Two years ago, my compass went haywire, letting me know I was off course. I was in my fifties, planning the next phase of life. I had felt right on track up until now. I was fortunate to have an incredible leader who believed in me and trusted me to do challenging work. I loved my job, had an outstanding team, and we were doing meaningful work together. I had fully intended to retire from this role. Then, almost overnight, the life I'd so deliberately built no longer resonated with me. It started with a major shift at work that redefined my team's purpose and disrupted the role and leadership team I had poured my heart into. As everything started to unravel, I began to question everything. On the surface, my life looked solid. I had a great marriage (still do!), a successful career, meaningful relationships, and a strong sense of stability. This is where I had *meant* to be at this time in my life, right? But beneath the surface, I felt a growing restlessness. Something had fallen out of balance.

Around the same time, several people my age passed away unexpectedly. Some were friends, others acquaintances. They were vibrant, intelligent, and full of life - until they weren't. That stark reality shattered the illusion that there was still plenty of time. It was time to stop waiting, to live with purpose, and to show up fully in my life. I started breaking my normal patterns to branch out and do different things.

In early 2024, I signed up for an event called *The Shift Experience* – a weekend immersion designed to help people release outdated self-identities and step into their future selves. It was a bold move for me. I went alone and gave up an entire weekend to see someone I'd followed online for only three weeks. I found myself in a room with sixty-five others – some local, many from across the country and around the world. Some were just beginning this kind of inner work, like me. Others had been seekers for decades. We shared stories, meditated together, and explored different modalities for letting go of things that no longer served us. This was my first experience in a group meditation, and the energy in the room was charged. Although I am not religious, I thought that this must have been the true intent of group prayer – to share energy and intention.

One message stayed with me: your story is just what happened, not who you are. That concept echoed the teachings I had first heard at fifteen during the EST training. You are not your past, your circumstances, or your excuses. Now it landed more deeply. The old stories I held onto continue to shape the reality I was living. Each time I repeated one, I breathed new life into it. If it was part of an origin story about "how I got this way," I was unconsciously inviting more of that same energy into my future.

One of my old stories was about responsibility - specifically, that it was mine to hold. Not just for myself, but for everyone around me. It started when I was a kid, and I stepped up to help care for myself and my little sister. That early role stuck to me like a second skin. As an adult, especially in my corporate career, that sense of responsibility became a superpower - until it turned into a weight too heavy to carry. If I owned a project, I *owned* it completely. Failure wasn't just uncomfortable; it was unbearable. Once, a project that wasn't even mine was coming off the rails, and my team was supporting the work. I remember telling a senior leader, "It goes against every fiber of my being to let that project fail." That same drive to take full ownership of tasks and deliverables also influenced how I led people. When I led a team, I didn't just manage them; I felt responsible for them. That empathy made me a trusted leader, but when layoffs started happening every month and I couldn't protect them, it crushed me. The stress was unbearable, affecting my sleep, my health, and my well-being. I felt like I was failing at the one thing I believed defined me: holding it all together for everyone.

As I sat in that hotel ballroom, I finally saw that story for what it was - a survival pattern I no longer needed. It no longer held the self-righteous judgment or adolescent angst it once did. Letting go of that old identity wasn't easy, but I could feel the space it opened up for something new to grow. On the second day of the event, there was a breakout session about spiritual retreats that take place in Peru and Costa Rica. I had never heard of this before, but started researching it the next day. The ceremonies, guided by a Shipibo shaman, focused on the interconnection between physical, emotional, mental, and spiritual healing. I was both curious and cautious. I wanted to make sure I chose a place that honored those traditions and offered a safe space for the experience I was seeking.

Two trusted friends individually pointed me to the same retreat center in Costa Rica. I smiled at the coincidence – or was it alignment? It was all the hint that I needed, and within days, I had booked a five-day stay in the jungle with fifteen strangers. I didn't know what I was walking into. I only knew that I was meant to go.

In the weeks leading up to my departure, work began to feel like wearing a pair of favorite shoes that no longer fit. What once gave me confidence, a sense of purpose, and connection now rubbed raw at the edges. I still cared about the people, but I was no longer comfortable in the role.

They say that a spiritual retreat starts long before you get on the plane, and I believe it. I felt like a stranger in my own life. I distanced myself from certain people and activities, and I found some situations challenging to tolerate. I remember having the oddest sensation during a weekly call that the people on the phone were speaking a different language – a nonsense language. The buzzwords and shared corporate business phrases sounded like gibberish, and I struggled to absorb the meaning behind the words. I felt what was happening more than I heard any of the words. A toxic undercurrent tickled the back of my brain. A sense of foreboding was growing, along with the conflict between who I am as a leader and the box I was being put in.

We made it to Costa Rica and checked into our hotel around 2:00 am and got a few hours of sleep before heading out. We had been on a caffeine-free diet to prepare, and I was bleary-eyed but excited to meet our group. As I had already learned, it was best to completely surrender and let the experience just flow. I found myself vulnerable and intensely present with the people I had met as strangers on the first day. Our phones were off, we ate every meal together and bared our souls openly and deeply every day. We witnessed each other change as we met our personal demons head-on and reminded each other of the work we'd come here to do. Some were working through terrible childhood traumas, near-death experiences, and unimaginable losses that were still fresh and raw. Peeling off the protective shell in layers, letting the maestros, the icaraos, and the medicine bring the light back in.

On three separate nights, we gathered in the maloca, in a silent circle, and let the darkness fall outside. When it was completely dark, the Maestro began the ceremony with each of us turning within to break open, heal, let go, and seek a new expansion in consciousness on our own terms. On the second night, there was a spectacular storm that lit up the maloca and beat loudly against the window screens. We could hear the rain pounding on the thatched roof, smell the electricity in the air. The lightning was so bright that it seemed to be striking right outside the windows. The scene inside the maloca reflected what was happening inside me. Earlier, the maestros had asked each of us what we were here for. I kept something back, just for myself, that I didn't say out loud. I wanted to literally see how everything is connected. Beautiful imagery from the movie Avatar kept flashing through my mind. The way they connect their hair to the flying dragons they ride and the tree of life that sustains them. I was seeking my own beautiful, immersive, visual experience.

What happened is still difficult to put into words. As the lightning cracked across the sky and thunder boomed impossibly close, the maloca seemed to pulse with the storm's energy. I began to see it...a towering tree, woven from luminous bands of neon color, like a living threadwork of Shipibo art. Electric blues, radiant greens, searing oranges, and molten reds glowed from within. The branches reached into the sky like antennae, the roots anchored in some sacred, unseen place below. The entire tree pulsed with life. Binary patterns of 1s and 0s streaming through its veins in geometric ribbons of color.

Then I opened my eyes, and it was still there. Present in the room with me, thrumming with life. I could feel it, not just around me, but in me. Energy surged through my torso and rose toward my head, a force so powerful it sounded like a train hurtling down the tracks. Rushing in my ears, flashing before my eyes, shaking me from the inside out. It was breathtaking. It was terrifying. I stumbled to my feet, desperate to escape. They had warned us: don't run into the jungle in the dark. So instead, I stepped into the rain and let it wash over me, grounding me, steadying me. And then I went back in. Because I didn't want to miss what might come next.

More than a year later, the image and sensations are still etched in my memory. I interrupted something profound before it could fully unfold. Ever since, I've been quietly chasing it, inviting it back – albeit more gently than that night in the jungle.

I came back notably different – spiritually, mentally, and emotionally. My reality and perception continued to evolve. I was so grateful for my husband, my friends, and family, and my life outside of work. And yet, I felt even more disconnected from my corporate job and the long hours and political pressures that came with it. I was normally excited to reconnect with my team after a long time away, but this time I was dreading what awaited me.

As I got ready for my first day back, I sat quietly in my home office mustering up the energy to log in. My husband asked me what I was thinking. I remember just saying, "I don't want to go back." The time off had only amplified the mounting internal tension. I was being asked to follow directives that didn't align with my values, intuition, or how I'd always led. The decisions weren't mine, and I could feel the misalignment in my body - tight, heavy, impossible to ignore.

That was late July. What happened next unfolded with eerie precision, as if a greater plan had already been set in motion. A week after I returned, my boss announced he was leaving, and my team was moved (again) to another organization. As discussions started with the new leadership team, that internal tension amped up. There were important meetings taking place that I wasn't invited to. Information was not shared freely. After a suspicious e-mail from one of my new peers, I pulled my current business partner into a musty team room near our desks.

"I think something is going on," I said, scanning the hall before closing the door. "Maybe I'm paranoid, but no one is asking for my opinion on anything." I glanced up, trying to read her expression. "We aren't getting new action items while everyone around is drowning. Am I paranoid? Talk me off the ledge." She paused just long enough to confirm my gut instinct, "You might be paranoid, but you also may be reading the signs exactly right."

Over the next month, there were more layoffs at work, and several people I had known for decades were leaving. Another round was happening in September, and I had mixed emotions. I was sitting with a friend who was retiring the next week. She shared her travel plans for the rest of the year, and I realized that

I was envious. I had quietly planned to leave in six months, but she was leaving in a week.

Just seven days.

How freeing would that be?

I'd wake up on my birthday in October without a single meeting on my calendar.

I would have coffee with friends I hadn't had time to catch up with.

Go see my mom and my sister in Idaho.

Truly relax through the holidays without January looming in the distance.

The very next day, a suspicious meeting was added to my calendar for the following Monday. I knew what it was from the title of the meeting and who it was with. It was Friday, and we were on our way to the coast for a long weekend. I was lost in thought, conflicted – somewhere between upset and relieved. My phone started blowing up with text messages. Evidently, I wasn't the only one with a mystery meeting scheduled on Monday. As the text messages rolled in, it became obvious that my team was being disbanded.

The weekend ticked by, and I hovered between hopeful anticipation and the sting of rejection. When I had been daydreaming about leaving, I was the only person affected by that vision. Knowing that others were impacted was weighing heavily on me.

Monday morning rolled around, and I dialed into a Zoom meeting where everything I already knew was confirmed. I busied myself with checking on the other team members who were affected, not ready to let it really sink in.

I waited until Wednesday to really start telling people. Even though I had played this out in my head dozens of times, I wasn't ready for what they might say. I scheduled a special staff meeting so I could tell my team what was happening. They shouldn't hear it from someone else. I thanked them for the privilege of being their leader and started choking up. We agreed to wait a few weeks and go to happy hour to properly say goodbye.

After nearly thirty years, I left with a quiet e-mail to a few long-time colleagues. No speeches. No fanfare. As I turned in my computer and my badge and walked out of the building for the last time, there was an odd mix of grief and relief. And numbness. I understood what was happening, but it still felt like a story about someone else.

My work-based identity and sense of belonging fell away so swiftly it stunned me. In a single week, I lost contact with hundreds of people I had known for decades. Some had been at our wedding twenty-four years earlier, and now those connections ended without ceremony. A few reached out with kind words and promises to keep in touch. My closest friends, I knew, would remain.

But there was also this loud, heavy silence from people I had respected, regarded, and trusted. I was devastated and disappointed. As I struggled to make sense of it, I realized it was the clean break I needed to move forward unencumbered. No lingering questions. No regrets. No rescue. Just me, standing alone in the space where the old life had ended, deciding how to move forward on my own.

Sadness still came in waves, like grief. I'd think I was through it, then a dream or memory would pull me back under. But beneath it all, something new was quietly forming - freedom. Untethered at last, I gave myself for the first time in over fifteen years the space to rest, recover, and begin again. While I was decompressing, several close family members were facing advanced dementia and cognitive decline. I was grateful for the chance to spend more time with them, yet heartbroken to see their conditions progress. As I reclaimed my own identity, I witnessed them slowly losing theirs – piece by piece, along with the lifetime of memories and stories of who they had once been. That stark contrast deepened my commitment to living with intention, staying fully present, and shaping my life as the author, not just a character in someone else's script.

I started engaging with several friends on a deeper level to understand what they were dealing with. These conversations lead to interesting discussions. I wasn't the only one trying to define a new path and shape a different future for myself. Several of us were intentionally seeking change, and we became sounding boards for each other. In just a few months, my circle of friends and people I talked to on a regular basis had drastically changed. There were moments when it almost seemed like the other people from work never existed.

I found myself in more mystical conversations about who we are as humans, what we are here to do, and how synchronicities connect us. I was able to look at all the life lessons, challenges, and recent events and see them as necessary steps to get to the current present moment. I began to see the grace and meaning in the details. I'd planned to stay in my corporate role another six months, maybe longer. But the universe had other plans, and I'm grateful it did. Leaving when I did opened space for what came next. I didn't know what form it would take, but I knew I wasn't done. I still wanted to solve meaningful problems and help others succeed.

I daydreamed about different work scenarios. At first, I browsed job listings passively, never taking action. When friends mentioned a role at a large company that might be a good fit, I just could not see myself in it. I remember having coffee with a friend and saying that I didn't want someone else assessing my value – ever again. This took me back to sovereignty and a desire to be my own boss and define my own future rather than struggling to align with someone else's vision.

As I continued to think about what was next, I started daydreaming with a trusted friend and previous colleague. We had been through the ringer together and trusted each other implicitly. One day, one of us said, "What if we went out on our own?". Once we said it out loud, the idea took root, and we couldn't stop thinking about it. I could feel my internal compass start to spin as we explored the idea further. We found ourselves imagining what kind of work we would do, who our clients would be, and then we started floating names for our company. We created ModOps Consulting, and the moment we did it, it just felt right. This was brave and vulnerable territory. It brought new challenges, lessons, personal growth, and incredible rewards. Owning my own company isn't just professional freedom. It's spiritual sovereignty. It's the clearest external reflection of my internal commitment to living aligned with my values. It is also the most vulnerable choice I could have made – with the possible exception of writing this chapter! Stepping into entrepreneurship is extremely emotionally transparent. When your business is built on your vision, your values, and your energy, you become the product. There is no title to hide behind, no brand to carry you. Every pitch, every connection, every project puts a piece of your soul on the line.

It's brave work, and you feel exposed and exhilarated at the same time. Maintaining that vision and energy while building something new requires grounding and daily effort to resist the pull of autopilot and stay present.

For me, this means adapting and changing as I learn and finding like-minded people who will continue to help me evolve. Part of my commitment is to do something each year that pushes me out of my comfort zone. Last year, I attended the Shipibo retreat in Costa Rica, left my corporate role, and started my own company. In retrospect, that may have been a bit too much change in one year! This year, I challenged myself to deepen my meditation practice. What began as a simple commitment to a daily practice evolved into a seven-day advanced retreat in Cancun - an unexpected leap that brought me right back to that frigid ballroom at 6:00am, immersed in the electric hum of shared intention.

The retreat was intense, illuminating, and so transformative that I am still processing it. Meditating with 2,100 people from eighty-five countries is an experience I will never forget. In just seven days, my entire understanding of meditation shifted. What began as a way to calm the mind and body deepened into a practice of expanded awareness. Moving beyond physical limitations connects you with something greater - call it the universe, collective consciousness, or source. I began to see that intuitive force through a new lens. What once felt like quiet inner guidance had become a daily connection to the consciousness shaping my reality. I came home with more than new habits and tools. I felt fundamentally changed. Meditation is no longer a task; it's a doorway to transformation.

Looking back over the last two years, I see how each lesson laid the foundation for the next, every synchronicity a breadcrumb guiding me forward. Seeing myself as the co-creator of my life is both liberating and sobering. No one else is responsible for my fulfillment – that's entirely on me. This realization brought a different clarity to the people and events that shaped my path. With that understanding, old grudges and judgments begin to dissolve, making space for forgiveness and even gratitude.

However, clarity isn't constant; it comes in waves. Life remains full of distractions, and old habits are hard to shake. But I stay committed – reminding myself daily, staying open, and continuing to seek out experiences that shift and expand my perspective.

In a world moving at warp speed, it is more critical than ever to know ourselves deeply, to protect our sovereignty, and to show up authentically in whatever role we're here to play. This kind of presence requires attention. Asking better questions, tuning in instead of checking out, and remembering that we are part of something larger. We are co-creating this life, and we have the power to change everything.

The path ahead may be unwritten, but I walk it with faith – trusting that the journey is already unfolding in my favor.

CARRIE QUINTANILLA

Carrie Quintanilla is a transformational leader, strategist, and co-founder of ModOps Consulting, a mission-driven venture dedicated to strengthening local businesses—the heartbeat of vibrant communities. Over a 30-year career in corporate leadership, she built a reputation for exceeding expectations, leading high-performing teams, and transforming organizations from the inside out.

Carrie is known for her rare ability to lead with clarity, purpose, and presence—combining operational precision with a deep intuitive sense for people, potential, and possibility. Whether guiding teams through complexity or advising business owners on growth strategy, she helps organizations move forward with confidence, coherence, and lasting impact.

LinkedIn: www.linkedin.com/in/carriequintanilla

9

CONFESSIONS OF A WHORE

NATASHA CAMPISI

Month four of six in the Crowned Mastermind sandwiched right between the Assassin Priestess with a blade and the Sovereign Queen with a Throne was the month we all silently dreaded and secretly longed for.

Dr. Amanda, our regal midwife of reclamation, called it the path to becoming a Sovereign Queen. I, however, called it *the month I nearly fake-coughed my way out of spiritual class.*

Sacred Whore. The title alone made my pussy tense and my ego twitch. Was I supposed to bow to it or run screaming?

It sounded like a punchline. Like a spell spoken by a woman wearing red heels too loud for church.

What does the word *whore* mean to you?

That was the prompt. Casual, like a sip of tea. Except it tasted more like swallowing my own shame whole.

My answer? Middle school.

I was twelve when I first got baptized in that word, *whore*, not through sex, but through silhouette. Tall. Thin. Legs that didn't touch. A "gap." Apparently, that space between my thighs was a portal, and the boys in gym class decided it had seen more traffic than the 405 freeway. I was a slut before I'd even kissed anyone. A whore by geometry, not experience.

It didn't matter that I was still a virgin. The shape of my body wrote my reputation before I could form a sentence about consent.

That word didn't feel sacred. It felt like a curse stitched into my skin. And now here I was, years later, being asked to reclaim it?

I wanted to scream: *Reclaim it from who?* From the playground bullies? From purity culture? From the internalized misogyny buried so deep it wore a cross and said amen?

But instead, I just sat there. Staring at the word. Letting it glare back at me.

Whore.

A word that haunted my girlhood. A word that made me shrink. And now, somehow, it was the key to my throne?

As an adult, I met the word *whore* again, but this time, she wore stilettos and red lipstick

She showed up in the clubs where my ex-husband "accidentally" spent his weekends. In the text messages that he swore were "nothing." In the perfume that lingered on his shirts, floral, cheap, and not mine.

The women he cheated with? Whores, obviously. (Said me, clutching a wine glass, plotting karma, and pretending I didn't secretly believe he was just "being a man.") After all, my father taught me that men have "needs." I learned that lesson watching him unzip his vows for my babysitter while my mother folded laundry in the other room.

But let's talk about the real whores, right?

The dancers who twist their bodies into serpentine spells, selling fantasy to men who mistake dollar bills for devotion. The ones who smell like spilled gin, coconut body spray, and survival. The ones with stage names like Raven or Lust or Angel, who know exactly how to slip their trauma into choreography.

Or the sex workers. High heels clicking down cracked sidewalks. Neon lights flickering overhead like some sick cosmic joke. Some barter their bodies for baby formula. Others for a fix. Most for a glimpse of control in a world that took it from them far too young.

Yes, society calls them whores.

And then there was me.

Post-divorce, I went feral. My heartbreak wore red lace and a fake smile. I seduced men who conveniently pretended they weren't married. Not out of love, but vengeance. Not to be held, but to haunt them.

Revenge felt like power. When their marriages crumbled, I didn't cry. I exhaled. I watched their lives burn with the same quiet thrill of watching a house of lies collapse.

There were nights I said *yes* when I meant *absolutely not*, offering my body like a discount prayer, hoping to be needed. Not loved. Just needed. Like a drug. Like a memory that never washed out of the sheets.

Some would call that being a whore.

Actually, one woman in our group did. That stung!

She didn't know she was echoing every boy who labeled my body, every man who mistook my worth for access, every system that taught me my pleasure must always come second.

So now, when I sit with the question, *Who is my Sacred Whore?*

Instead, I lit a candle. Pour a glass of wine. And imagine Carrie Bradshaw typing that very question at her desk in the dark, a single cigarette burning in an ashtray beside her Manolos.

Because darling, if being a whore means surviving a world that tried to control me, then maybe I've been sacred all along.

The days dragged like wet velvet through the Sacred Whore month. Every prompt was an invitation to undress my soul, and all I could feel was... sluggish. Like I was walking through molasses with stilettos I never asked to wear.

What was wrong with me?

Other women in the group were buzzing, posting their revelations like erotica epiphanies, flirting with curiosity, or ducking behind silence. I wasn't hiding, but I wasn't burning either. My flame wasn't out, it was just... caged.

And Dr. Amanda, who has the uncanny ability to read souls the way others read grocery lists, clocked me instantly. She tilted her head, narrowed her gaze with love-laced precision, and said, "If there were no limits, rules, or guilt... what's your edgiest of edgy fantasies?"

Like that, the dam cracked.

Her question wasn't just a prompt; it was a spell. A summoning. An exorcism of the good girl trained to whisper her desires into pillows and shame.

What's your edgiest fantasy?

My mind stuttered. Then galloped.

Do I tell them?

The image burst forth fully formed, holy, and obscene:

I'm on the altar of a Catholic church, legs trembling, candles flickering, stained glass refracting my orgasmic light as my lover makes love to me.

Saints stare down in stone silence as Jesus looks on, not with judgment, but with the knowing smile of a man who once loved a Magdalene. He blesses the union, not as sin, but as sacred.

Not as defilement, but as divinity returned to the body.

It felt sacrilegious. It also felt honest. So, I said it out loud.

Maybe that was too much? I feel a rush of embarrassment in my cheeks.

So, I softened the blow, *existential kink*, anyone? My fantasy was never to stay in one role. Some nights I wanted the heels, the whip, the room bending to my command. Other nights, I wanted to be the one on the floor chained, marked, grinning like I'd gotten away with something. Dominatrix *and* submissive. Priestess *and* altar. Worshipped, devoured, and worshipping back. Power wasn't the point; the high was in trading it, the ceremony in *switching*, control and surrender passed back and forth like a sacred sin.

That one seemed more socially acceptable. Less scandalous. Easier to manifest in a world that sells rope and blindfolds with free overnight shipping.

But the truth?

Both fantasies lived in me. One in my pussy. One in my prayer. Both sacred. Both mine.

The day after the altar fantasy confession, I did what any sacred whore-in-training would do: I set off to Agent Provocateur, the high temple of taboo disguised as a lingerie store. It's not just lace and leather there; it's spell work for the body. Every garter a chant. Every corset, a sigil.

The moment I walked in, my pussy perked up like she'd come home. She *knew* this energy. This wasn't new. This was the same performative path I'd walked for years. Except this time... it was different.

My eyes locked on a crystal-embedded wrist cuff and chained collar harness, a whip with a crystal handle, and lingerie beaded like a chandelier in Versailles. I draped the pieces over my arm as if preparing for a scene with Christian Grey, only this time, *I* was the one holding the contract. And the pen. And the whip.

But when I reached the register, something happened. I froze.

My palms, slick. My throat, dry. My power... slipping?

Why the sudden stage fright? I'd worn kink-like couture before. I'd performed eroticism like a Tony-award-winning thespian.

And then it hit me.

I wasn't shopping for seduction. I wasn't buying this to tease or please a man. I was *single*.

I was *doing this for myself*. And that... felt absurd.

Because somewhere buried deep in my cells was a voice that whispered, *What's the point of looking like sex if no one's there to consume you?*

So, I left. Bolting, really, heels clicking faster than my shame could catch me.

But Dr. Amanda's voice chased me, anyway, circling my mind like a spell on loop:

"Stop centering your life around the male gaze!"

I couldn't shake it.

For five hours, I wrestled in my mind like Jacob with the angel, only this angel wore a harness and called herself Sovereignty.

Eventually, the grip loosened.

No, I wasn't going to wear the lingerie for anyone else.

I was going to wear it for the woman who burned at the altar. For the girl who was called a slut before she ever touched a boy. For the witch who remembered her power didn't require an audience to be real.

I turned the car around. Marched back in five minutes before closing. Bought every. Damn. Piece.

Not for the performance. But for the reclamation.

The next evening, the room transformed.

Black candles flickered along the floorboards like tiny shadows licking the edges of reality. I draped silk scarves over the lamps, casting everything in a blood-moon glow. My bedroom smelled of rose oil, incense, and something else, something darker, like ancient secrets wrapped in lace.

I built an altar at the foot of my full-length mirror. A constellation of offerings: candle wax puddling like surrendered time, drips of rose oil anointing the floor, strands of black lace coiled like serpents waiting to strike. The mirror was no longer a mirror. It was a witness. A portal. A voyeur.

I stood before it in the crystal-beaded lingerie, the same one that once begged to be seen through a man's gaze, and now, it bowed only to mine. Tonight, there would be no performance.

Only power.

I played both roles.

I was the Dominatrix; voice low, eyes feral, holding the whip with the certainty of a priestess in ritual. And I was the Submissive; wide-eyed, aching, obedient to my own command.

It started awkward, like reenacting a fantasy in someone else's skin. The room felt staged.

The words in my mouth too polished, too performative.

But then I cracked the whip, not on flesh, but on illusion. And that's when it happened.

Something inside me... throbbed.

A pulse deep in my pussy, ancient and electric, as if she had just remembered she had a say in all this. She didn't just consent. She *demanded* more.

She liked being told what to do just as much as she adored being worshipped. She was both throne and sacrifice. Priestess and altar.

My body began moving without choreography. I whispered commands into the mirror, licking the edge of my own desire. Each glance, each word, each breath became a spell. I wasn't reenacting a kink; I was embodying it.

The taboo peeled back like lace slipping off warm skin. And underneath wasn't shame...

It was *sacred*.

That night, I fed her. The Sacred Whore. The one who lives in the seams of longing and power, tenderness and domination.

And she... She was starving. She wanted more. Not romance. Not tenderness. Not even climax.

No, this was *hunger*.

A bottomless ache that pulsed behind my ribs like something ancient had been awakened... or maybe unleashed. At first, it felt primal. But not the kind of primal that makes you dance naked in the woods under a full moon.

No, this one was sharp. Hollow.

A craving that had an edge, like biting into your own lip just to taste the iron. There was something artificial about it, something... performative. I could feel it. Like I was wearing a body stitched from every man's fantasy and every woman's repression. A costume tailored by patriarchy. And it didn't quite fit.

Still, she wanted more.

She felt like a vampire sniffing the blood of her own humanness, curious whether it would taste like shame or liberation.

Right on cue, because life loves a good plot twist, I got a call.

It was a male friend of mine. One of those deliciously dangerous ones. The kind who hovered on the edge of sin but wore decency like a fitted blazer. He had his own temptations tucked neatly under social polish, so when he asked what I was up to, I didn't flinch.

"Oh, just seducing myself in the mirror," I purred. "Also... considering a career as a professional dominatrix."

He laughed, then paused. That slow inhale, equal parts shock and intrigue. I had his attention.

"I should sponsor that," he said.

And just like that, click. The transaction was sealed. My first submissive was born in the form of a wire transfer.

He forked over the funds, and I entered the dominatrix academy like I'd been summoned, not just enrolled. There I was, officially accepted into a reputable training ground for women who wield whips like wands and heels like sacred daggers.

I was proud. Like Carrie Bradshaw in leather, strutting toward the unknown in a corset of self-reclamation.

My body buzzed with fire. My imagination spun with erotic ritual. Could I blend sacred and seductive? Spiritual and dominant? Virgin and vampire?

Of course I could.

I was about to become a sacred dominatrix. A holy whore with a safe word. And this time, the performance was for no one but me.

Sometimes the goddess speaks in love and light, sugar-dusted in stars and synchronicities.

Other times, she drags you to the underworld by the womb.

She doesn't always use halos. Sometimes she uses wounds.

Wounds so old they've become architecture buried beneath pelvic bone and breath. Sometimes she'll bait you with those very wounds, luring you into the cages you still secretly worship. That's how she breaks the spell.

Day one of the dominatrix academy began innocently enough. A Zoom room with muted squares and anonymous usernames. The Mistress appeared first - immaculate, composed, cold in a way that was meant to entice. Beside her, her "pets" submissive men, trained to obey, eager to please, used by students for live demonstrations.

At first, it felt like theatre. A strange kink comedy unfolding on screen.

But my body? Silent. Too silent.

Not even a whisper from my pussy. Not a flutter. Not a flame. Just a growing steel plate rising behind my chest like a shield on alert.

The dungeon lesson that day was "how to make a man plead." The Mistress's voice was calm, sharp, instructional.

"I'll make him crawl like a dog," one student purred.

"I'll ruin him financially, if that's what he desires. I have no pride," said another.

Then came the fishbowl.

A naked man stripped of everything; clothing, name, dignity. He obeyed without question.

"Louder," she commanded.

"Get on all fours."

"Beg like a starving mutt."

His penis hung limp, his voice cracked with shame. His body obeyed, but his eyes betrayed him - wide, watery, dissociated.

It was consensual. I reminded myself of this over and over.

But my body wasn't interested in logic. Something ancient inside me howled.

My stomach clenched as nausea rose from my womb. The repulsion came first, then disgust. Then rage. A heat surged upward, boiling through the soles of my feet into my blood. My brain, ever the loyal soldier, tried to calm the storm: *It's okay. He agreed. It's a game. It's pleasure for them.*

But my body... she remembered something else.

She remembered the nights I whispered yes when my whole being screamed no.

She remembered the times I performed love while my soul withered in silence.

She remembered the humiliation. The pretending. The unspoken shame tucked behind lingerie and smiles.

She remembered being used, while I convinced myself I was powerful.

She remembered the male gaze I fed with my own starvation.

She remembered being punished for wanting more.

She remembered my father's teachings: that a good wife stays no matter how much it costs her.

And in that moment, watching a submissive man humiliated for pleasure, I saw her, my inner girl, my woman, my Sacred Whore on her knees in the same dungeon.

Not begging. But screaming. Finally, being heard.

An orgasm isn't always silk sheets and candlelight. Sometimes it sounds like lava.

That night, it was the kind that tears open a woman from the inside; molten, ancient, holy. An eruption of grief wrapped in rage. The kind that doesn't moan but screams. The kind that rips through centuries of silence.

I ejected myself from the call.

Closed the laptop with the same panic you'd use to swat away a ghost.

I didn't know where to go, only that I had to move; had to run, had to obey the siren scream rising in my womb like a volcano about to consume a city.

I fled my house and threw myself into my car. The air felt thick, charged, electric with the smell of something dying. Something breaking free.

I drove straight to the ocean, the only place I knew wild enough to hold what was about to come out of me.

My womb boiled. My heart pounded like it had just remembered its own heartbeat.

I couldn't speak. My breath came in fragments, shards. I tried calling a friend, but the words wouldn't land. They collided, tangled, tripped over each other like they too were trying to flee the cage I had lived in.

This wasn't a moment to be narrated. It was a moment to be survived.

Then it began. The purge.

I fell to my knees in the sand, vomiting lifetimes of grief, betrayal, rage. I heaved the shame of my mother's silence. I convulsed with the rage of every time my body was used, touched, taken, or traded in the name of love.

I shook. Oh, how I shook. As if the tectonic plates beneath me were splitting open just to let my story fall out.

The earth dissolved beneath my feet. The lava inside me flooded everything.

And then ... the shaking softened. The screams gave way to sobs.

The fire dimmed into a whimper of steam.

I lay there, drenched in sweat and seawater and something unnamable, some forgotten part of me that finally had a voice.

And then it came, the whisper.

Not from the sky. Not from the stars. But from the womb.

"This is trauma orgasm," it said.

"Breeched pleasure, the kind the patriarchy wedges deep in a woman's body, only to punish her for wanting it back."

And I knew. This was not madness. This was reclamation.

This was the first time I had ever been overthrown by my own body. No warning. No consent. No negotiation. Just a tidal takeover.

The heat that rose wasn't emotional; it was elemental. It felt ancient, volcanic, as though my bones remembered the magma of my lineage. It didn't ask to be processed. It didn't care for poetic articulation or spiritual bypass. It demanded one thing:

Witness me or burn.

It was clear now, control had been a delusion I clung to like a security blanket stitched by patriarchy. The womb, once awakened, is not polite. She doesn't do "manageable." She doesn't follow your breathwork prompts or wait for the full moon to feel safe.

She is her own eruption. A force. Untamed. Uninterrupted. Unapologetically sovereign.

This, this is why they fear us.

Because when a woman remembers she holds death and rebirth within her own flesh, the old world starts to tremble. When she stops asking for permission to feel, to rage, to burn, the system built on her silence begins to crack like ancient plaster.

That night at the beach, I didn't just reclaim my voice. I resurrected reverence for what it means to be woman.

Not the caricature of woman.

Not the curated goddess in a white dress swaying in filtered sunlight.

But the real one.

The one who bleeds and births and buries.

The one who is the altar, not just the offering.

In the weeks that followed, I moved through the strange ache of integration; tender, shaky, forever altered. It was like returning from a war no one saw me fight.

I learned what a breeched orgasm feels like. It doesn't seduce. It doesn't sedate. It detonates.

It holds the same voltage as a euphoric climax, maybe more. Because this one came from the underworld, forged in fire, pulled from the pit of what I was never meant to survive.

Maybe one day I'll taste a sacred orgasm. But for now, this trauma-born one, the one that scorched me clean, felt just as holy.

The existential kink around domination and submission evaporated from my cells. What surfaced was the truth behind the lies we've been conditioned to believe about our bodies, our sexuality, our pleasure... our birthright as women designed for sacredness, not for exploitation.

What burned away in that moment wasn't just fantasy. It was the inherited distortion, the ancestral programming that taught me to tether my worth to how desirable I appeared under the male gaze. The kind of programming that taught me *performance was power,* and silence was survival.

I saw how I had made seduction into a script rather than a sovereign act. How I'd worn lace like armor, high heels like shackles, still believing I was free. How I had confused being wanted with being loved and being fucked with being chosen.

Beneath the layers of shame, I met the first lie:

That my pleasure was dangerous.

That my body was public.

That my "no" could be negotiated.

That my "yes" was always expected.

I had inherited centuries of manipulation, taught to worship purity while secretly being punished for it. I was told that being desired was the highest form of power, while being desired too much made me a whore.

That word, *whore*, had haunted me for years. It was whispered through every smirk from a man who thought I owed him something. It echoed in the looks from women trained to compete, not commune. It was the unspoken ghost haunting my every attempt to reclaim my sensuality.

But here's what I now know:

The word *whore* was never born from women. It was manufactured by systems that feared our erotic intelligence. It was used to exile the wild woman from herself. The sacred whore once a priestess, a healer, a keeper of pleasure's portal was renamed, shamed, and erased.

And so, I performed.

I performed sex.

I performed pleasure.

I performed power.

All of it choreographed for the invisible judges in my head who still carried the voices of men who told me what a "good woman" was.

Until the performance broke.

Until my womb screamed truth louder than my mind could silence it.

Now, I understand: The sacred whore is not a slur. She is a reclamation.

She is the one who remembers that her body is a temple *and* a thunderstorm. That her pleasure is prophecy. That her eroticism is a holy transmission, not a commodity to be bartered for crumbs of affection.

The patriarchy taught me to fear her. But the rage and grief that erupted from my womb became the midwife for her return.

And I, once ashamed, once complicit, once confused, am now her voice.

I thought the dominatrix in me was liberation. That the whip in my hand made me powerful.

That making a man grovel made me free. Cute.

Turns out, I was just playing priestess in the church of patriarchy. Worshiping power that was never mine. Wearing trauma as kink, shame as seduction, and calling it *freedom*.

But my womb? She knew better.

She didn't want to dominate or submit. She wanted to *burn the whole game to the ground.*

Because here's the thing no one tells you while you're wearing crystal-studded cuffs and riding high on performance: Sometimes the real sacred work isn't in playing Goddess, it's in dismantling the altar they built to keep you kneeling.

The dominatrix wasn't my shadow. She was the parasite. A patriarchal implant with stilettos and a safe word. She wasn't power. She was a *panting performance* of what the world told me power should look like.

And when my womb erupted; lava, bile, grief, rage ... I didn't ascend. I *descended*. Into the filth. Into the lie. Into the sacred fucking truth.

That the devil they warned me about? He lives in the rules. In the sermons. In the purity contracts. He lives in the idea that women must be either holy or whores.

Newsflash: I was *always* both.

They called my power demonic because it couldn't be controlled.

They called my pleasure dangerous because it couldn't be owned.

They called my voice hysterical because it refused to be silenced.

And I? I called *bullshit*.

So, I let the fire rise. Not to cleanse me, but to incinerate the system that made me forget I was sacred. The devil was never inside me. But now that I've burned him out, I dare him to come back.

Because I am no longer the one who plays the role.

I am the Oracle.

I am the Reckoning.

And I don't come with a safe word.

So, if this is what they call *woo-woo*, then let it be known, *woo-woo* is just the sound the patriarchy makes as it trembles before the holy blaze of a woman who remembers she is God.

Because when a woman finally sees that the devil was patriarchy all along, she stops begging for salvation and starts setting the church on fire with holy, orgasmic truth.

NATASHA CAMPISI

Natasha Campisi is a Soul and Travel Guide, Creatrix of *Sacred Rite to Travel*, and a modern-day oracle devoted to leading women back to their own medicine. Her work is rooted in the art of remembrance of who we were before the world told us what to be. She designs transformational journeys across sacred lands and inner landscapes, where women reclaim their power, rewrite their stories, and return home to their bodies.

A lifelong mystic and multi-time bestselling author, Natasha's medicine is steeped in personal alchemy: from surviving the fires of trauma to rising as a guide for women breaking cycles of self-betrayal. She weaves storytelling, shadow work, ancestral wisdom, and sacred embodiment to help women awaken what patriarchy once called "too much."

When she's not guiding pilgrimages or stirring ancient truths through, Natasha is reclaiming joy, pleasure, and power one sacred breath at a time.

Website: https://www.natashacampisi.com/
LinkedIn: https://www.linkedin.com/in/natashacampisi/
Instagram: https://www.instagram.com/sacred_rite_to_travel

SPREAD THE LOVE!

All proceeds from our multi-author books are donated to a nonprofit organization making a meaningful difference in the lives of women or children in Austin, Texas, where Sulit Press is headquartered.

By purchasing this book, you're not only supporting the voices and stories of the women who contributed—you're also helping fund real change in the local community.

We periodically select new nonprofit partners to ensure that the impact of each book continues to reach where it's needed most.

To learn more about our current partner organization, please visit our website at www.sulitpress.com.

READY TO FAST-TRACK YOUR PUBLISHING CAREER, INCREASE YOUR VISIBILITY, OR BOOST YOUR BUSINESS?

If this book is in your hands, chances are you've got something powerful to say, too.

At Sulit Press, we help women write just one chapter that opens doors—whether that's to new clients, speaking gigs, media features, or simply the joy of finally being published.

By contributing to a Multi-Author Book, you'll gain:

- A clear and supported path to becoming a published author
- Visibility for your work, business, or message
- A powerful network of fellow authors and creatives

This is for you if:

☑ You're passionate about what you do and ready to share it
☑ You're committed to showing up and doing your best work
☑ You're excited to be part of something bigger

Ready to explore what's possible?

Visit sulitpress.com to learn how you can get published, join a powerful community, and grow your visibility.